Praise for *Beyond Worksheets*

"This book provides powerful paradigm shifts for educators. As a lifetime global educator, Amy is able to weave practical ideas with transformative outcomes. A must-read whether you've been teaching one year or fifty."

—*Sarah Gould, Ed.D.,*
Global Education Practitioner and Researcher

"Moving away from worksheets is not about discarding all structure; Amy does a great job of explaining this; instead, she talks about creating a learning environment that fosters collaboration, critical thinking, and creative problem-solving. By replacing passive learning with active engagement, we empower students to become not just consumers of knowledge, but creators, collaborators, and leaders in shaping the future . . . which are the essential skills for success in a rapidly changing world today."

—*Kevin Hodges,*
Texas, K12 LCS Lead, Google for Education

"At a time when education faces a crisis of engagement and relevance, Amy Mayer's *Beyond Worksheets* emerges as a beacon of hope and transformation. This pivotal book directly addresses the urgent need for a paradigm shift in teaching methods, championing innovative yet practical, learner-centered approaches to design meaningful, personalized, and awesome experiences for every learner."

—*Christopher Bugaj,*
M.A. CCC-SLP

"Amy Mayer has a wonderful ability to transform personal experience and stories into deeply practical tips and strategies for fellow educators. *Beyond Worksheet*s is full of reflection opportunities, activities, and action steps that will help any teacher lean into the instructional challenges that we commonly face in schools."

—*Scott McLeod,*
Professor of Educational Leadership,
University of Colorado Denver; Founding Director, CASTLE

Beyond Worksheets

Beyond Worksheets

Amy Minter Mayer

JB JOSSEY-BASS™
A Wiley Brand

Published by John Wiley & Sons, Inc., Hoboken, New Jersey.
Published simultaneously in Canada.

For general information on our other products and services or for technical support, please contact
our Customer Care Department within the United States at (800) 762-2974, outside the United States
at (317) 572-3993 or fax (317) 572-4002.

Wiley also publishes its books in a variety of electronic formats. Some content that appears in print
may not be available in electronic formats. For more information about Wiley products, visit our
web site at www.wiley.com.

Library of Congress Cataloging-in-Publication Data

Names: Mayer, Amy Minter, author.
Title: Beyond worksheets : creative ways to teach and engage students / Amy
    Minter Mayer.
Description: First edition. | San Francisco, CA : Jossey-Bass, [2024] |
    Includes index.
Identifiers: LCCN 2023056405 (print) | LCCN 2023056406 (ebook) | ISBN
    9781394200115 (paperback) | ISBN 9781394200122 (adobe pdf) | ISBN
    9781394200139 (epub)
Subjects: LCSH: Creative teaching. | Motivation in education. | Educational
    change. | Creative ability—Study and teaching.
Classification: LCC LB1025.3 .M34453 2024 (print) | LCC LB1025.3 (ebook)
    | DDC 370.7—dc23/eng/20231214
LC record available at https://lccn.loc.gov/2023056405
LC ebook record available at https://lccn.loc.gov/2023056406

Cover Design: Wiley
Cover Image: © Lumos sp/Adobe Stock
Author Photo: © Patricia Berry
SKY10072526_041524

Contents

Introduction

I wrote this book with the hope that it will inspire teachers who, when they are told not to use worksheets or that worksheets are "bad," secretly think, "But what else is there? How do I have students practice in an organized way without worksheets?" Whether a school is trying to get beyond worksheets because of copier click limits or ideological incongruities, the question for teachers remains, and it deserves an answer. How do I restructure my classroom and the learning taking place within so that worksheets will naturally die? The question this book seeks to answer is: "What do I do instead?"

The death of worksheets, for me, came naturally. I didn't start out my career having any idea what to do instead; in fact, I started out knowing nothing. After two years of teaching public school, or should I say being paid as a public school teacher, I still didn't know much about what else to do besides hand out worksheets, take up worksheets, and grade worksheets. Thank goodness, I guess, that I was mostly an English teacher so that at least students were writing something from time to time.

Looking back now from such a distant vantage point, I recall the thrill I felt when I found a CD for sale online with quizzes and questions (worksheets) for just about every classic novel you can think of. I used that thing until the lasers wore the shine off the disk. I mean, I modified the content for my students, but that CD was the starting place for just about everything. Thinking about having students read x, y, or z? That depends; is it on the CD? So, what was wrong about sending kids home to read a chapter or two then peppering them with written questions on the daily? Nothing much except, come to find out, hardly any of them were actually reading any texts except SparkNotes, by then ubiquitous and free online for almost any piece of literature, and actually a pretty good resource. The problem wasn't just that, though; it was that what I should have been teaching and what I wanted to teach, and what I MEANT to teach could not be taught in that way. Inadvertently, what I taught instead was how to fake it through reading checks, not how to enjoy, or even understand, literature. For the most part, only I was having a good time. Not to defend myself too much, but everyone I knew was pretty much hinging their lesson plans on the same premise. Honestly, most teachers still are. The problem is, we don't know what else to do besides what was done unto us. An interesting perversion of the golden rule: "Do unto others what was done unto you" instead of "Do unto others what you would have done unto you."

Eventually, I "taught" a class that instead taught me several thousand valuable lessons about motivation. I applied those lessons pretty promptly to my "on level" students, but I failed to make a bridge to my Dual Credit charges. I tormented them with the worksheet methodology throughout my public school career. I got better at writing questions, and eventually, abandoned the trusty old CD (yes, before CD players in computers stopped being mass produced). Sometimes as I look back on the whole of my teaching career of both those over and under 18, I think every single thing I've learned is really about one thing: motivation. It's much easier to learn about curriculum and instruction than it is to understand how to create the motivation to learn that most students have to have to achieve diddly squat beyond what they came into the room knowing how to do. As you might have guessed, neither the CD nor the content I created to emulate it in future years took into account motivation beyond the most basic transaction students and teachers make, also known as grades.

Ironically, if grades had mattered to even 50% of the students I taught, I never would have had to become the master manipulator that made other people say I was a great teacher or that allowed me to be an adult professional educational development provider company owner. As Arthur Ashe, legendary American tennis player, famously said, "Success is a journey, not a destination." How true those words are. Throughout much of my teaching career, I would have told you that I longed for students who cared about my opinion of them or about the grades on their report cards, but you know what? In most ways, those are the easy ones. I'm not saying I didn't come to love many of those little grade grubbers dearly, but I am telling you that they are not the ones who taught me to question every little thing I thought I knew about education, every little thing that had been done unto me, every little thing that, in former times, I would have told you education was about. Thank goodness for the other ones. The ones who came to school dirty and disheveled. The ones who didn't have front doors on their trailer houses. The ones who needed school to be good and to make them care about it more than I had ever needed anything.

The first time you read this book, I hope you will do so in order. I hope the stories and examples make sense in the order they are placed. Later, I hope you go back to chapters when you need them. In the future, there will be a course that accompanies this book, which will be available in our learning platform called friEdOnline (Fried Online, located at http://friedonline.com). In most chapters, you will find a connection to technology that not only makes sense, but also inspires you to either try replacing a process you currently have in place with something that will, once thoroughly learned and adopted, be categorically better than what you had before and save you time and effort or to increase engagement with your students. You'll also find periods to reflect. I have to admit, in college education classes, I wrote a lot of "reflections" and I grew to hate them very much. I thought they were another form of busy work (and they were) that professors gave out when they didn't know what else to do. No one read them. Once I figured out I was just filling pages with drivel no one but me would ever read, I had a lot more fun with them, and ironically, that is actually a good point. Reflections should be for the learner themself, not necessarily for another audience. I can 100% confirm regarding those college assignments that NO ONE READ THEM because I would have had some awkward comments if they had. But, now, I see reflections differently. Whether you write them down or just take time to think your thoughts about my message and your reaction to it, that is the beauty of two minds melding in the way that only a book written by and read by a human being can. So, please take a minute to yourself when you reach a reflection and let us commune in thought together about a profession that is precious enough to you to read a book and to me to write one.

Giving Up the "Good Old Days" of Education

I want you to take a moment with me and picture the first school that you attended. You might not remember the layout of every classroom, each teacher's name, or who you played with at recess, but I would be shocked if you don't remember the pride in seeing a drawing you worked tirelessly on taped up in the hallways, the sound of the intercom buzz for morning announcements, or the smell of the cafeteria emanating through the halls at lunchtime (to me, elementary schools always smell like canned green beans). For so many of us who have spent our lives in the field of education, we chose this path, not only due to our own success as students, but because of these memories and the comfort that we can so easily find in a school environment. Those walls that we remember fondly haven't changed much. In fact, if you haven't moved from your hometown, it is likely that the same school building where you attended is still in use today. Many school buildings have been used for over 100 years, but even for schools that have been built in recent years, the layout, intention, and design of the school has not changed significantly. There are a

1

few notable trends that briefly threatened the larger trend (anyone remember open concept schools?), but even then, the mental constructs that continue to define the life of a school have, for the most part, remained unchanged since the one-room schoolhouses went away and the "factory model" of schools arose. If you were to suddenly wake up in a classroom one morning, you might not know much, but you would know that you were inside a school right away. While these mental and physical constructs of the space haven't changed beyond our recognition, the daily lives of the students who inhabit those hallowed halls is likely an entirely different story.

At the age of six, I started attending what was the only elementary school in my small hometown, Livingston Elementary School. My family's communication structure fell apart one day when I was about nine, which meant there was no one there to get me as I stood outside squinting to try and pick out the family car. I know that I was probably less than a mile from my grandparents' house and a half mile away from my mom's job at the town's library, but none of that made me feel much better. As a child, it was scary. So scary I can't even remember now how I solved the problem. I think someone at the school called one of my parents and obviously (thankfully) I am not still there. Someone eventually came and picked me up, but I will never forget the way I felt. This was another time, there were no cell phones, I had no money to use a pay phone (had there even been one), and I certainly wasn't prepared to hoof it on the side of the road. I already had significant general anxiety, which was thrown even further out of proportion due to this incident. So much so that when my own daughter started school, I knew that I needed to talk to her about what to do should this ever happen to her. With me at the helm, I knew it was definitely a possibility. So I asked her, "Sylvie, if no one picked you up from the bus stop or at school, what would you do?" She was calm, completely missing the implied anxiety behind my question,

"Um, just call you on my cell phone I guess?"

Oh . . . oh, yeah, I guess you would just do that, wouldn't you? SO MUCH has changed in the world between 1980 and 2005. The ubiquity of smartphones was a powerful part of that, but it certainly was not the only thing. As I write this in 2023, it's been a shocking 43 years since I was nine years old wondering what to do after school. But nevertheless, my school experiences somehow happened that long ago. I'm not trying to upset you. What I am trying to do is to make you think about how long it's been since you were that age, what memories and experiences you might be bringing with you to your career as an educator, and how the changes that come with the passage of time can and do completely alter the life of a student now compared to then, even if "then" for you is more recent than for me. It's unfortunate that memories don't yellow like newspapers, giving a better hint of their age. My childhood must have been just a few weeks ago and has to be filled with relevant, accessible memories of school that I can use. Except it wasn't, and it's not.

Even with all of these changes, schools have largely remained the same in substance and in form. Even some of the most damaging aspects of school have remained the same as when "we" were growing up, no matter how long ago that may have been. Policies forced down through systems, like No Child Left Behind (instituted in 2001), have been impacting public education systems with standardized testing requirements for practically as long as I can remember. I graduated from high school in 1990 in Texas, home of the standardized test—thank you (but no thank you), Ross Perot. I believe my senior class was the first to have the requirement of passing a test in order to graduate, at least that's what we were told, and it seemed to play out.[1] The test was of minimum skills and most everyone I knew passed easily. There was no test prep in advance, and as I think back, I don't even think we knew the test was happening until the day it was given. (Contrast that to the deeply embedded high-stakes testing environment of today and you will long for the "good old days" with good reason.) I only remember one classmate of mine not being able to pass a portion of the test. I had attended school with her on and off since first grade. I'd been to her house, seen her at parties, and considered her a friend. It was stunning to think she wouldn't be able to attend graduation over a test we hadn't even heard about before it happened and that none of our teachers decided to give us. Never before had we encountered a test that had such an impact on our educational careers. I didn't realize it at the time, but it was the end of an era in education, an era where schools decided who did, and did not, graduate; at that moment, then and to this day, the state, at least in my home state of Texas, had thoroughly and finally wrested that control from the school district.

What Do We Mean by "the Good Old Days" Anyway?

Through the lens of the introduction of standardized testing, I do sometimes long for the good old days. There is another kind of "good old days" I think we can often refer to in the mythical past. There was a time when children sat quietly in rows, everyone had enough to eat at home, and no one's parents said curse words on a daily basis. Each child was taught what the "bad" words were, *everyone* spoke English, and when the school called home, the student was the one in trouble, not the teacher. Teachers were expected to "cover material," and students either got it or didn't, at no apparent fault of the teacher. The understanding was that it was there if you wanted it, or if you didn't, that was a "you" (student) problem if you couldn't keep up. This is the version of "the good old days" I was thinking of when I began this chapter. The nostalgic past where we had nuclear bomb drills that required holding a hefty textbook cracked in half over your head. The world where a hefty textbook could either teach or protect you from doom, clear proof that words held power.

This world demanded a level of conformity and homogeneousness that appears not to exist now. (Did it ever? I probably don't know because I was a member of the "in" group.) We all *had* to agree on what the bad words were AND that they were, in fact, "bad." We *had* to see the systems as "in charge" and students and parents as supplicants to those systems. These are just a couple of minor examples of the agreements that had to remain in place for that old system to be sustained. When I hear educators long for the good old days, I always think about what they really mean. I think part of it is the relaxation of living in a world where white middle-class privilege is so firmly in place that it cannot be called into question. The world we're picturing might have seemed better for everyone, when in fact, it was only better for some. Not to be too heavy-handed about this point, but I think that this quote brings it home:

> "Better never means better for everyone. . . . It always means worse, for some."
>
> Margaret Atwood, *The Handmaid's Tale*

Journaling Activity

Close your eyes and picture your quintessential school experience using all of your senses. What does it smell like? What do you hear? How does that metal seating that we somehow all had feel?

Grab your favorite notebook, a scratch piece of paper, or whatever is closest to you that can be used to write on (the margins of this book also work just fine, I promise I won't be upset!). Writing it out, take this moment to name and reflect on what each of your senses immediately recognizes when thinking about your school experience. Then, think about how these spaces may have changed or remained the same in the years since. This isn't an essay to be graded or an assignment to turn in, so write as much or as little as you would like. There are no wrong answers!

Make sure to keep the paper you used close, as we will reflect back on this once more at the end of this chapter.

If the "Good Old Days" Were Good, Why Should We Leave Them Behind?

Thinking back to those days that I keep referring to as the "Good Old Days," a world that, at one point, I would often get nostalgic for, I have come to realize that I had no idea that I was living in the midst of privilege. Poor as we were, I still had a privilege that was making life impossible for so many others while creating a cradle for me. Because of this insight that I now have, I cannot, in good conscience, continue to wish for the "Good Old Days." I now understand that these days never truly existed.

Nostalgia in education is longing for a world where only some of us could prosper, so as chaotic as the world of education may seem now, at least there has become room for so many more voices, ways of being, and an overall more equitable experience, though we still have so far to go. I don't want to pretend or even imply that life is now easy for those who come to public school from poverty, or for those who are different from what many may still call "normal" in any way. (What is "normal" anyway?) However, a child who is transgendered, for example, has a chance today to be treated with dignity, although it may still be an uphill battle, there would have been no chance in the elementary school I attended in the 1980s.

As another example, a child whose native language is not English will undoubtedly have a better chance for a "free and appropriate education" (to which every child is entitled under federal law regarding students with disabilities) than they would have in 1985, 1995, or even 2005.[2] Much more is understood in our school systems about the many varieties of inclusion, acceptance, and how instructional practices can increase opportunities for more students. A student who is in need of special education services would also have a better opportunity to encounter a learning environment where they may grow today than in the "you get what you get" learning environment norms of yesteryear.

So, in hindsight, the "Good Old Days" weren't that good; we still have a long way to go, and no one has all the answers. As chaotic as schools may seem today, we may be closer than we ever have been to true equity and inclusion in the diverse world we find ourselves in today.

Evaluating Your Learning Environment

For those of you who are teachers or administrators, you are probably starting to wonder, "If school is so much better for so many, why is it so much worse for me?" One answer is that schools are no longer, for the most part, organized solely around the needs of the adults who work there to be good places to work. Please do not think that I am saying schools are only for students; at their best, schools form communities, and at times, safe havens for the adults who work there as well as for the students who attend. So there is a problem here too: how do we create a school environment that serves all students equitably as opposed to equally, giving each what they need instead of everyone getting the same, while still providing a happy and healthy working environment for the adults who also populate the buildings? It is time for designers of systems to figure out how the needs of students can best be met with the adult resources that are available without burning those adults out. Schools cannot be everything to everyone, at least not with the funding any system in the United States has dedicated to it. I have worked in private schools where parents pay $40,000 a year per student and in the poorest school district in the state of Texas; in neither of these organizations was there ever "enough" time or other resources for educators. Although, I have to admit, the private school was a much better environment for adults than the public one. Conversely, the public one was a much better environment for a student with special needs than the private one.

A thought experiment that I think has a lot of value for educators is to figure out where their school falls on the continuum shown in Figure 1.1.

Let's take a look at an example that will help you think through how to evaluate your learning environment, whether it's a school campus or a school district (group of schools).

In our imaginary scenario, as so often in real life, yet another mandate has arrived from the state: all students classified as "at risk," that is, identified as living in poverty (qualifying for free or reduced lunch), who have been identified as homeless, who failed the state standardized assessment in the last three administrations, or have met one of a bevy of other identifiers, must have three extra

Student-Centered	Centered	Adult-Centered
Solutions are designed around the needs of students, no matter the consequences for adults.	Solutions are designed to have the most benefit for students considering the available staff resources.	Solutions are designed around the needs of adults, no matter the consequences for students.
Potential Example: Montessori Elementary School		Potential Example: Freshman lecture course at a university

FIGURE 1.1 Student-centered versus teacher-centered schools.

hours per week of instructional time with a highly qualified teacher. In our fictional district, although this is often the case in many real districts around the country, there is little or no funding for extra personnel to carry out this mandate. Those "highly qualified" teachers are already at their wits' end with the existing work and now all eyes are on them to somehow provide these "extra hours."

How will the learning environment and school community address the mandate? Thinking through how your school would address it will tell you everything you need to know about whether you are working in a mostly student-centered environment, a mostly adult-centered environment, or if you are one of the lucky few who are at some healthy place in between (how did you do it?!). I've taken the liberty of talking through how I think each type of system would address this mandate as follows.

In a mostly student-centered learning institution, conversations will revolve around who gets the services and what the services will be. Definitions may even be expanded locally to include more students than required or use more time than is required by the mandate. Educators may look at how they can accommodate student needs for extended transportation. Meaning they, or some other adults, will be spending extra hours after the end of the school day with students instead of accomplishing all of the other work they usually do during that time. An assumption may be made that the services will be provided in small groups with a human teacher or that this content will be created by each teacher taking part. Art, physical education (PE), lunch, and recess will probably be off limits unless there are extreme extenuating circumstances because, again, the assumption will be made that students need these subjects, wouldn't want to miss them, or would feel punished by doing academic work during these sacred "non-academic" time periods. In the student-centered model, the problem may be restated like this: At-risk students need expanded instructional time.

To contrast, in an adult-centered learning environment, conversations will first revolve around excluding as many students as possible from receiving additional services. Next, rules will be examined to see how many students can be accommodated at once and how few adult resources can be dedicated to meet the requirements of the mandate. One or more pieces of software may be procured to help with the work and to decrease the load on staff. Decision-makers may also examine the rules to see when the services can be delivered with the least amount of additional strain to the adult system, for example, at lunch, during PE, music, art, or during other "elective" subjects. In the adult-centered model, the problem may be restated like this: The state says at-risk students have to spend three extra hours a week doing schoolwork.

The problem with the completely student-centered approach provided is that it may not be sustainable, in which case decision-makers will have to go back to the drawing board no matter how "good" their solution is for learners. While the students' needs are kept front and center, if there are not enough resources to consistently provide the services, then what "good" is really being done? The problem with the completely adult-centered approach is that the underlying reason for the extended services (most likely to raise test scores or to "catch up" on lost learning) may trump much of the potential joy a child experiences at school without regard for that quite important facet.

As an interesting aside that ties into this thought experiment, a colleague of mine did an informal study once. They took a look at mandatory student tutorials and test scores and found that for boys who were forced into after-school tutorials, scores actually dropped versus girls whose scores remained stagnant. Neither group of 5th graders benefitted from thousands of hours and dollars spent to try to "catch" them up. My theory is that the instructional practices used in the initial instruction were the same ones used during the "extra" learning time. They didn't work initially, so they also didn't work just because they were done more frequently or for longer periods of time. At any rate, if you are part of a discussion around extending instructional time to combat learning loss, it's worth noting that a proposed solution may pose no benefits for either students or adults. Ask questions and look at data before finalizing any plan of action.

Now, let's get back into our scenario. A balanced approach must: address the need to comply with the mandate, serve the students receiving the instructional services meant to help them, and be sustainable by the adults required to provide these services. If your school has a centered approach, I hope you are seeing decision-makers work with classroom teachers to design solutions that solve problems in creative ways. For example, can classroom teachers work with art, music, or PE teachers to integrate learning in new and different ways to address the underlying problem of learning loss? Can services be expanded in ways that will raise up all of the learners while meeting the requirements of the edict? Are people thinking through how to make school better for everyone, adults as well as students, when "problems" like this arise? Or is only one of the two groups involved in this extra learning time being considered? In the centered model, the problem may be restated like this: At-risk students need expanded opportunities to address learning loss without impinging on the work/life balance of highly qualified teachers.

Dealing with Mandates from On High

Dealing with the adversity of working within a monolithic system teaches us about who we are as individuals and as educators. Here's a quick guide to dealing with the ever-expanding mandates from on high that might lead to more centered, inclusive, and balanced outcomes:

- First: What problem are we trying to solve?
  - Before diving in to find a solution, play around with how you frame the problem you are experiencing. How the problem is framed is going to determine how you approach solving it and your flexibility in finding solutions. Problems can, and should, always be framed in multiple ways before a solution begins to be developed.
  - Example of a well-stated problem: Some students need expanded learning time delivered in new ways in order to achieve maximum growth.
- Second: Is there a way to address the problem that benefits more or even all students?
  - Here, we would ideally take into account the entire student experience, including but not limited to: the

workload a solution would add to what may already be a full plate for a student, the social implications the proposed solution could have in a student's life (such as missing out on important bonding time during recess), and how the proposed solution could affect a student's life outside of the classroom or school building (e.g., more homework is likely not the answer).

- Example of a proposed student-centered solution: We will create an integrated art and music program where students are learning academic skills while creating with different mediums. This solution could benefit all or at least more students while solving the restated problem.

- Third: Is there a way to address the problem using adult resources respectfully?

  - Just as we took the entire student experience into account, we should take the entire teacher experience into account. We should look at areas such as: the workload the proposed solution could add for the teacher, how the proposed solution could negatively affect other duties educators have at the school, and how the proposed solution would impact an educator's overall work/life balance.

  - Example of a proposed teacher-centered solution: Hosting a volunteer design committee to think through ways to address the problem (NOT just the mandate) with various stakeholders present which could yield exciting results. This work needs to be done during the school day, so substitutes will be required. Potential volunteers need to understand how their work may be impacted by the decisions of the design committee so that they can volunteer based on their interest once they understand the stakes. They also need to know in advance about any potential commitments outside of the regular workday. The more student-centered the learning environment has been, the more assurances will need to be made that the needs of adults will be respected within the design process.

Using "Design Thinking" strategies[3] to deal with mandates can cause a major cultural shift for learning institutions. We don't have to cut up paper hexagons and play with pretend issues to consider how to solve problems effectively. (Design thinking means understanding the users of a system and gaining empathy for each role involved so that the solutions devised work for everyone.) We DO, however, have to let go of the TTWWADI (That's the Way We've Always Done It) if our learning institution doesn't have a history of balancing student and adult needs. Killing the TTWWADI is the first step toward getting Beyond Worksheets, which is presumably why you're reading this book in the first place. Though I realize, even as I type this, that some of you have been told you MUST read this book and ironically have been given little, or maybe even no, information as to why. If this is the case, I am truly sorry, but hope you will still enjoy it. It's time for you to be the voice of reason and initiate balanced practices, to the extent that you are able with the resources you possess, in your own institution of learning.

Strategies and Tools for Improvement

If you change nothing, nothing changes. In a study that examined educational needs post-pandemic, Yong Zhao and Jim Watterston[4] found that curriculum post-pandemic needs to be developmental, personalized, and student-focused. Additionally, the researchers suggest that capitalizing on technology such as synchronous (all together right now, live) and asynchronous (individually on your own time at your own pace) learning is critical for students to be proficient in the rapidly changing world. My goal is to give you tool suggestions and strategies to implement after each chapter of this book. So these sections are meant to give you ideas for concrete implementation in your own classroom, school, or district. I'm a big believer in small incremental monthly changes throughout the school year, which can build into changes that are larger than the sum of the parts. As you look back on your school year, wouldn't it be nice to know that you did something new and different each month? For example, I like to make November the month of forms and celebrate a time I like to call *Formsgiving*. Everyone implements ONE form into one of their existing workflow processes, and then we can share our forms with each other. Happy Formsgiving! My hope is that each of these chapter closers can give you some ideas for how to move forward, month after month, with one small change that could add up to make a big difference.

Forms and Shortened URLs

This first Strategy and Tool add-on will focus on implementing digital forms at every level of your school system, from central office to the classroom. Forms are powerful tools that can be used to crowdsource information and fuel your design thinking processes. You might have heard this quote before: "The smartest person in the room is the room," and thank goodness there are now a bevy of technical tools to make gathering those ideas possible.

There are a million different forms services out there that can help you create beautifully crafted, multilayer forms, but I always suggest starting with the basics (remember, many small changes can be just as powerful, if not more so, than a few big changes). If you have access to Google or Microsoft in your school, you have an easy way to gather data from anyone with a few clicks. It is important to note that this book is not meant to address what those clicks should be, what forms would help you most, or the ins and outs of process creation. Both of these companies have loads of free information online addressing each of those clicks and how they can be utilized today (even if you are reading this book years after it was released). Not to mention the avalanche of professional development services that would eagerly host an engagement centered on these forms and their uses. My job is to give you ideas and templates addressing why you might want to use these tools and how to actually complete the process of sharing the forms with your constituents, whether those are administrators, parents, or the students in an elementary classroom.

Here are some ideas for how you might use forms for some different audiences:

Student-Facing Forms	Staff-Facing Forms

Incorporate forms directly into the learning process:
    One example would be to teach students how to use forms to write "choose your own adventure" stories. Then, have their peers read the stories multiple times, making different choices on each read through to experience the full story. As a bonus, you could gather story feedback for the authors through forms as well!
    Template/Example: https://fried.tech/bw-adventure
	Give staff a voice:
	    You could make your next staff professional development day an EdCamp style event by crowdsourcing session ideas then asking for crowdsourced expertise instead of traditional presenters. (Did you know that over 90% of educators polled said unstructured EdCamps had changed their practices?)[5]
	    Template: https://fried.tech/bw-edcamp-form
	    I love this blog article by Pam Hubler about how to implement a school-based EdCamp: https://fried.tech/bw-edcamp-schoolpd

Student-Facing Forms	Staff-Facing Forms

Make it engaging:
    Poll the class about whom they would like to invite as the next virtual guest speaker for your classroom. Then, use the data you collect in the form to try to persuade the speaker to talk to your class. As a bonus, you could review an anonymized version of the data with your students to teach about data analytics, tie the voting process into a learning unit on politics, and show them how their opinion was valued and used in real life.
	Make it relevant:
	    Plan a staff appreciation event with real data after asking teachers what would fill their buckets and make them feel appreciated. Maybe it's candy or a drink from Sonic, but it also might be a sticker or pen. Ask the staff about their employee "Love Languages" and use the data all year to fill those buckets.

Use them as a form of feedback:
    Ask students how they want to display their learning or how they learn best. This will give you new ideas for how to best connect with students and to create new ways to understand their learning. As a bonus, you could have a constantly open form that allows students to submit ideas, concerns, fears, or general feedback throughout their time in your classroom! (Be sure to turn on form notifications for this one.)
	Show them how forms can be problem solvers:
	    Use forms to solve problems that haven't even happened yet by creating forms. For example, if there is a fear students might see something "bad" on the internet, create a form to gather the data when there is a problem. If the problem happens, you'll know and can deal with it. (Be sure to turn on form notifications for this one as well.) AND if it's a "made up problem" that's used to try to generate fear, you will have the "data" or lack thereof to prove that the problem is not as big as some might believe.

Forms are doomed to fail if we use them as an additional "thing" that students or teachers have to do beyond their normal work. We should instead use forms as a solution to existing problems, which will help to drive engagement and change the culture around how a classroom, school, or district uses forms.

Think about it; you spend hours creating a form for a new engagement opportunity and send out an email blast. You get a few responses immediately, a few more over the next week, and then submission comes to a halt. Since this task was just another "plus one" that had to get done, it did not become part of the existing system. So how do we get the link to the form to the people who need to fill it out in such a way where they continue to engage with it? This can be daunting, especially when a one-time email blast won't suffice. Here are some workflow ideas that may help you share the link to your form in a meaningful way.

First, make sure the form settings will allow your audience to complete the form (and turn on multiple submissions if it is a form where one submitter may submit many responses); consider whether they will be required to log in or not, for example, and change your form settings accordingly. For example, if my audience does not have the ability to log in, I do not want to use the "automatically collect email" setting because they will not be able to complete the form. I should turn off that setting and then ask them to type in their email addresses in a text field response.

Next I have to think about how my users can receive the link to the form. If I have their email addresses, this is fairly easy. I can copy and paste the link right into an email. However, if my users are 2nd graders without email and I don't have a Learning Management System, I can still use forms if I know how to use a URL shortener. Here are a few tools that shorten URLs you may have heard of:

http://bitly.com

http://tinyurl.com

Each of these tools works similarly. You copy the long web address (or URL) and paste it into one of the tools. Hit "go," and it will spit out a short version of the long URL. Both Bit.ly and Tiny URL have the ability to customize those short links or use the default random link. With both services, the custom link you want cannot have been used before. I like to think of initials for whatever project I'm working on that can be appended before the link. For example, links for this book will start with bw, making them unique, so each short URL starts with bw- (short for **Beyond Worksheets**, the title of this book) then a word or words to describe the link. Short URLs can be printed out, written on white boards, or projected on screens in the classroom. Anyone can access them depending on the settings of your file or form. Some services also give you the ability to generate a QR code, which is like a short URL that devices with cameras can read. You probably know how to use them since they became so ubiquitous during the pandemic, especially for restaurant menus! From a user perspective, open the camera app on the device and let the camera "see" the QR Code. The camera will pop up a URL (web address) on the screen. Click on or tap the web address to visit it. Both Bit.ly and Tiny URL can also generate QR codes for your links. It's often handy to provide both the QR Code and the shortened URL to the user, then if one doesn't work, you have a backup. QR Codes and shortened URLs can be displayed using a projector or screen or printed out on paper.

It is worth noting that some school systems may not allow their teachers or students to use the websites I previously mentioned. However, there are many other services that will allow you to accomplish the same goal. If this is something that you are interested in using, but also know your school has a policy against, I would encourage you to work with your administrators to find a similar service that they would approve for use. It may be that they have a trusted tool (such as Adobe Express or Canva Education) that you could start using today.

By the same token, you should also examine short URLs before you click them if you are getting them from an unknown or as yet untrusted source. Each major link shortening service has a way to check its own short URLs before clicking on them or you can use a site like https:// checkshorturl.com/ to expand and examine a short URL made with just about any service. Why do this? Because "bad actors" can hide scammy and spammy links by using URL shorteners and get you to click on them and install software on your computer or phone that can do things you do not want, like record your keystrokes (i.e., everything you type) or allow them to activate your webcam, and so on. While I never want anyone to NOT use technology out of fear, if you are inexperienced with it, you need strategies to protect yourself and your students so that you can move forward with confidence. If this is a topic that interests you, be sure to check out our online course called Safe and Secure. You can find it in the friEdOnline catalog at this long (and safe) URL: https://www.friedonline.com/. As a security measure, you should always be wary of short URLs that come via email; if someone is emailing you a legitimate link, they can just link the text you see or send you the "long" link on which you can just click. There are, therefore, not many good reasons to use a short URL within an email except to try to make text appear to be something it's not.

Reflection Activity

Take out your journaling activity from earlier in this chapter. Now that we have talked about the "Good Old Days," learned about student-focused, teacher-focused, and centered systems, and discussed strategies with how to navigate these systems, I'd like us to take some more time to reflect.

Knowing what you know now, think about the changes you see between that picture you remembered of your school experience and how schools look today. If you had to guess, were these changes made in order to create a more student-focused, teacher-focused, or centered system? I would challenge you to take it a step further and think about a change you or your school system has made recently (we know changes are the only constant!). Was this change made for the students, the teachers, or was it that magic combination of truly serving both groups? It is my hope that you will start asking these questions every time you are involved in helping to make change. It will undoubtedly serve you well.

Takeaways

1. The most powerful influence on how we do things now is our own past experience. By examining our past with adult eyes, we can get past the nostalgia that may otherwise keep us stuck.

2. The way forward can be neither entirely "student centered" nor entirely "adult centered"; instead, the way forward must balance the needs of students and educators.

3. Using forms to gather data can be a powerful practice for capturing the voices of everyone to make the best informed decisions possible.

Notes

1. Susan Chira. (1992). The 1992 campaign: Shaking the schools; when Perot took on Texas—A special report.; Education Initiative Revealed A Savvy and Abrasive Perot. *New York Times*

2. Free appropriate public education for students with disabilities: Requirements under Section 504 of The Rehabilitation Act of 1973. (1999). https://www2.ed.gov/about/offices/list/ocr/docs/edlite-FAPE504.html

3. Rebecca Linke. (2017). Design thinking, explained: Ideas made to matter. https://mitsloan.mit.edu/ideas-made-to-matter/design-thinking-explained#:~:text=At%20a%20high%20level%2C%20the,through%20the%20customary%20deployment%20mechanisms

4. Yong Zhao and Jim Watterston. (2021). The changes we need: Education post COVID-19. *Journal of Educational Change* 22: 3–12.

5. Jeffrey Paul Carpenter and Jayme Nixon Linton. (2018). Educators' perspectives on the impact of EdCamp unconference professional learning. *Teaching and Teacher Education*. https://www.sciencedirect.com/science/article/pii/S0742051X17312374

What Is a Worksheet?

I first used the words *Worksheet Killer* on my Twitter profile many years ago; I liked the irony; as a child, I actually enjoyed most worksheets quite a bit. In fact, I could "kill" a worksheet in short order. Give me a packet and I would complete it in what I felt was record time and worthy of high praise. (Although I hated the math ones, the rest felt like games.) I liked the worksheets because I could do them. However, once I "grew up" and became a teacher, I eventually saw the dark side:

> The child who needs the worksheet can't do it.
>
> The child who can, doesn't need it.

Take a moment and let that concept sink in. From my younger, more egocentric perspective, worksheets were great. But once I re-joined the school environment as an educator, I had to look at the problem of worksheets from a completely different angle. What were my students, like one I'll call Jolene, doing with all those worksheets? They certainly weren't bringing them back completed like I had asked them to! But why not? Why was something that I saw as an almost joyful part of my educational experience falling flat? I got my lesson early on, which began my understanding of why worksheets can't work. This chapter explores that idea, and we'll begin considering strategies and tools we can use when we pretend the worksheet doesn't exist.

The Story of Jolene

First, I want to begin, nearly at the beginning, of the experiences that taught me that teaching cannot be automated or routinized in the way that worksheets require. In my first year of teaching in Conroe ISD in southeast Texas, I met Jolene. Jolene was a polite child who looked older than her years. She was someone you might call "world weary." She wore her inexpertly dyed red hair in a ponytail every day with blonde white roots prominent around the edges of her scalp. Her clothes were repetitive, wrinkled, and often smelled of cat urine. Nevertheless, Jolene was a sweet kid who I enjoyed having in class. I certainly worried about her success and could not understand why neither she, nor about 95% of my other students, would do any homework, even if it made them all fail. In my own life as a student, homework was understood to just be a part of the deal. I would have never known that there was a world out there that precluded homework. One day, I decided to ask Jolene what the deal was because I could tell she felt embarrassed about not having her homework. Based on my interactions with her, it was pretty obvious that she would do anything to please me. Honestly, I think she was probably the only one in her class who felt that way, so she seemed like a good case to help me understand the disconnect.

I pulled Jolene aside one day and asked her why she didn't do her homework when she was such a good student in the classroom. She said something like this: "Well, I have three younger siblings and right now we live in an RV we are borrowing from one of my mom's boyfriends. My mom works at night, so it is up to me to figure out how to feed my younger brother and sisters, try to get them cleaned up, and then get them to bed. Once I get all that figured out, it's dark and I can't see to do the work because we don't have electricity. I tried getting up really early to work on it, but, Mrs. Mayer, I'm just too tired and my mom gets really mad if I wake her up before we all have to get up to get ready for school. Plus, in the morning, I have to get my siblings up and ready to get on the bus and, well, it's hard. It takes a long time, and, well, maybe I'm just not very good at it."

I could tell that Jolene felt embarrassed to tell me this, and I felt even worse for having asked it. I wish I knew where she was today so I could thank her for helping this middle-class child-teacher understand what was so obvious that it astounds me now that I even had to ask. The truth was, I had never contemplated a world where a 15-year-old girl would have to feed, bathe, and otherwise care for three children by herself. I'm an only child, and while we didn't have much, we sure never lived in an old RV without any electricity. It was my second year of teaching in a high-poverty school, and I started thinking back right away about how many punishments and zeros I had doled out to former students who probably had lives very much like Jolene's at home. All of those kids who I didn't ask "why" began to line up in my memory. I felt terrible, but there wasn't much, or anything really, that I could do about the past. So instead, I focused on what I could change, the future.

Another thing I now realize that I should have been asking myself was this: If those worksheets mattered at all, and Jolene had never turned in one of them, why were her other performance measures satisfactory? Why was she passing tests, quizzes, and even state standardized assessments? If the worksheets mattered at all, why was her writing steadily improving, and so ultimately, why was I giving them out in the first place? The answer was really pretty simple. As teachers, the most powerful influence on any of us is our own schooling experience. It's sad but true. The first, and most powerful, lasting learning experiences I had about teaching began in the late 1970s when I started my schooling as a student. Throughout all my years of primary and secondary education, I had done worksheets both during class time, mostly when the teacher needed a break, and at home. No one questioned this process. Homework, by and large, was a worksheet. If the school was running low on funds, we might even have had to copy the worksheet onto notebook paper and then hand the purple copy (that's right, before photocopying machines, copies were purple) back to the teacher to be used again with their next class. They would come numbered, precious artifacts as they were. But why were they precious? Why did we do them at all? Was there any aspect of them that was important for learning? And where did all those worksheets even come from anyway?

After my conversation with Jolene, whom I now felt I understood better than any other student I had taught up to that point in time, I began to think more critically about the work students were asked to do in my class. I wondered, and analyzed in depth, whether the work was actually contributing to their ability to critically read and understand texts or to write clearly and comprehensively. I had to start getting honest with myself. Anything that could be measured by a worksheet was clearly not contributing to those goals because those goals, even if the texts were the same, were a bit different for each individual student. Was there really any reason all of them had to be reading and understanding the same exact passage or story? Sure, that's how it would be on "THE TEST" of all tests, for we were (and are) in Texas, the home of the standardized test. But, who cared? If you had the skills to read and understand, then you could read and understand most anything. Might it be better for students to be choosing texts, or for me to give them a range of options, or even better, for them to be creating new texts themselves? Could it possibly be more impactful to construct one's own questions than to have them written for you? Well, of course, it was! This all seemed pretty daunting. However, once I changed my viewpoint about worksheets, one insidious form of standardized assignment, I found new and exciting ways of practicing the skills that were profoundly superior. As it turned out, the more I did that, the more worthless I found worksheets to be. As a bonus, I found that my "copy clicks" went way down and my students' grades went way up when I stopped trying to assess their ability to do work from home. I found that assessment of work completed at home, as it turns out, was much more an assessment of their parents' abilities to construct a stable home environment than anything else, and measuring that was neither my job nor my intention.

That Christmas, Jolene surprised me by bringing me a gift. This child, who had nothing to her name, found a present for me and even a box to put it in and brought it to school. It was a little gold Christmas ornament depicting the Nativity scene. I cried when she gave it to me, and I cry again every year, even now 25+ years later, when I put it on the tree each holiday season. I remember Jolene, the struggles she faced, and that I never saw her again after that school year. I often wonder what happened to that kid who began teaching me everything I needed to know about worksheets, especially as homework. I hope she found her way out of that life of dire poverty that was so different from mine.

What Is a Worksheet?

Let's take some time to think about what elements make the blameless document what we're calling a *worksheet*:

- **One-Size Fits All:** A worksheet is the same for everyone, making it (theoretically) easy to grade since the answers should all be the same or nearly the same for everyone, and thus, it may falsely be perceived as a timesaver for the teacher. But remember, if an activity or assignment is not helping students learn, whether it is done in the classroom, at home, or on the bus ride to school in the morning (as is often the case for many students), it is instead wasting everyone's time.

- **It's Basically a Test, NOT an Instructional Method:** A worksheet is much more like an assessment than it is like a practice session. It assumes the doer already knows something about some specific content in a subject area that they are now expected to reproduce a multitude of times. Some examples could be, "Spot the object of the sentence," or "Do these 50 times table problems." If a student does not already have the background knowledge of how to find the object in a sentence, or does not already know the times table or at least how to work out the problems, they are sunk. The document isn't teaching the skills, it's assessing something they are supposed to have already learned during classroom instruction. Now, some might say, "It's important to practice though! That's what worksheets are for." But if a student already knows how to do something, why do they need to do it 50 times? And if they don't already know how to do it, how will they do it 50 times? What if they do it wrong 50 times?! Wow, now they have really learned how to do it wrong! Over and over! I think we often lean on the phrase "Practice makes perfect," when in fact, it could be said that "Practice makes permanent." These students who are practicing the wrong way begin to be hurt by these worksheets we were not so sure were a good idea in the first place. I hope you are starting to understand the conundrums worksheets can create.

- **It's Busy Work:** Many times, a worksheet is used as busy work. I think all of us, or at least most of us, can agree that busy work is work that benefits no one other than being a tool for eating up spare time. People feel it deeply when they are asked to do busy work, and the older and more intelligent they are, the more angry and disengaged it makes them. The No. 1 battle cry from beleaguered teachers today is "there is not enough time," so one would think that eliminating this giant time suck should be a welcome relief from tedium for both students and teachers. If you're reading this and you are a teacher, you might be feeling a little over-whelmed or panicky right now, and it might be because you don't know what to do tomorrow in class besides a worksheet. You may even have a colleague who retired long ago who left you a bevy of materials you've been hanging onto like a life raft. Those materials are probably worksheets or even workbooks/packets, which are just names for ways to package many worksheets together. You may also be thinking that your school or district requires a certain number of grades in the gradebook. Worksheets may be where your students' averages are mainly coming from and they may also be underpinning your lesson planning. If any of this rings true for you, then have no fear, you're in the right place. In this book, I hope to give you many ideas of how to think about creating assignments in ways that will benefit your students so much more than any worksheet or other exercise of busy work possibly could. Your students' skills will grow faster and stronger when they are engaged in working on something that is much more meaningful, interesting, and individualized than a worksheet.

It might help to remember for a second before we move on that what we presumably wanted when we were assigning that worksheet was for students to learn a skill they would be able to apply, not just to get a grade into the gradebook (although that would be a nice addition if you work in a school with a minimum number of grades in a category that is difficult to achieve).

Journaling Activity

Take a moment and think about a worksheet that you have either completed as a student or assigned as a teacher.

Writing it out, take this time to detail the parts of that worksheet and how they relate to the three components of a worksheet I previously described. What about the worksheet felt good when it was originally assigned? How does it feel now looking at it through this new lens? Do you think you would be excited to assign (or be assigned) this worksheet knowing what you do now? Make sure to keep this journal entry close, as we will reflect back on this once more at the end of this chapter.

To put your mind at ease, I want us to go through an example together. Let's take a learning objective, examine a worksheet that we used to think was addressing the learning objective, and then look at how to get students creating in order to learn instead. Let's go ahead and tackle something hard, inferencing. I think any of us who have taught an English and Language Arts class can agree that inferring is one of the hardest skills to teach. Here are two examples of standards about inferencing from the 6th grade:

Standard example 1: "Students understand, make inferences and draw conclusions about the structure and elements of fiction and provide evidence from text to support their understanding."[1]

Standard example 2: "Cite textual evidence to support analysis of what the text says explicitly as well as inferences drawn from the text."[2]

The mockup shown in Figure 2.1 is an amalgamation of worksheets I found online by Googling "6th-grade inferencing worksheet."

As you examine this worksheet, I think you will agree that it meets each characteristic of our definition:

1. **One-Size Fits All:** The same for everyone and easy to grade.

2. **It's Basically a Test, NOT an Instructional Method:** This worksheet is definitely more like an assessment than actual

(Continued)

practice. (If I don't already know the skill, how could I possibly be able to do it?)

3. **It's Busy Work:** While this worksheet will take time to complete, it will not advance the students' knowledge of inferencing in any meaningful way. It can only hope to provide evidence of whether they have already mastered the skill or not.

Name:_____

Class Period:_____

Instructor Name:_____

Inferencing Practice

Read the passage and then answer the questions below.

> Jeanine enjoyed baking pies on the weekend almost as much as her brother enjoyed eating them. One weekend, Jeanine ended up having to bake a second pie after the first one went entirely missing nearly as soon as it was baked. No one in the family had a clue what had happened to it; she asked each of them! Jeanine left the pie cooling on a rack next to the stove in one of the disposable pie pans she favored so that she could give away her pies and not have the worry of the pan being returned. That evening, Ronnie, Jeanine's younger brother, had a roaring stomachache. After the disappearance of the first pie, a blueberry dream, Jeanine had no choice but to bake another one; she was committed to bringing something to her family's Sunday dinner. Strangely enough, Ronnie showed, for the first time ever, no interest in eating dinner or having pie at the family get-together. Their mother worried Ronnie was seriously ill, his lips were bluish and his skin coloring was a bit green. She wondered aloud if she should take him to the urgent care clinic. Jeanine solved the mystery that evening when she took out the trash and found the empty pie pan barely hidden within.

Who does Jeanine think took the pie?_____

Provide evidence from the story to support your answer:

1. _____

2. _____

3. _____

FIGURE 2.1 Example worksheet on inferencing.

Through my experience, I now know (deeply) that creating in order to learn is the most profoundly effective way to truly grasp new skills. If a person can create something, even if they are researching and gaining new knowledge during the creation process, they are more likely to understand and retain that knowledge. In fact, this is true especially if they are researching during the learning process. This is a profoundly different exercise from consuming and regurgitating information, which is all that can be asked on a worksheet.

Practicing Getting Beyond the Worksheet

Let's take a look at an alternative assignment about inferencing at this URL: https://fried.tech/bw-inference

In this exercise, students are actively reading and getting real practice at inferring. Most teachers would demonstrate analyzing the first incredibly short story together. It might go something like this: The teacher reads aloud one of the stories, for example:

> "Fire truck!" yelled five-year-old Billy. His mom had told him his dad was a fireman. When he got older he set fires, hoping to meet Dad.
>
> *Credit to Sean Hill for submitting this story I found on*
> http://www.sixwordstories.net/ *years ago.*

In a whole-group setting, the teacher may then ask each student to think about why Billy became an arsonist. In this case, most students will realize that Billy thought his dad, the fireman, would make an appearance at one of his fires. "Why did he think this?" the teacher would ask, and someone may answer that because his mom told him his dad was a fireman, Billy assumed he might be one of the firefighters who responded to the fires Billy created. In this model of teaching though, only one of the students is probably answering any one of these questions. That may be okay as long as everyone knows that, in a few minutes, they will be writing a story individually and sharing those stories with their table groups. It's critical we're all thinking about extremely short stories and how they're constructed as well as what role inferring has within such a short story. We also have to consider that we know we're going to need to do something and that there will be an audience for later. All of this knowledge creates the "need to know" that helps me, and many of my previous students, stay engaged in the work; plus, we know this part of the work is fleeting. Soon, we'll be asked to do something with what we're currently thinking about.

Next the teacher may start a release. Perhaps now table groups will read the next few stories and discuss them within their smaller groups. More people will be speaking now, which is a pathway to learning for many of us. The teacher may provide some questions for each table to use if conversation falters. These could be shown on a projector or written on the board while the table discussions are happening. The teacher can now walk around the room and listen to the discussions. This will give students the chance to correct misunderstandings or ask more probing questions to facilitate deeper discussion. The conversation starters could be something like these:

1. What do you know about the narrator of the story and how do you know it?

2. What is the inference you have to make in order for this story to make sense?

3. How do you know the inference you drew is correct? (What evidence is there from the text that supports your inference?)

4. How much do you think the photos displayed with the stories are changing your perceptions of the stories?

In the story of Billy and the firefighters, for example, we know that the narrator is not part of the story; he is not Billy, Billy's dad, or Billy's mom. What we do know is that the narrator knows why Billy sets fires. Second, the inference we have to make is that Billy believes he will get to see his father if he sets something on fire so that the fire department has to make an appearance. We can infer that this is Billy's motivation because he's been excited about fire trucks since he was at least five years old, and later on, sets things on fire. The only evidence we have of why is that his mother has told him his dad was a firefighter. The textual evidence here that supports this inference is "His mom had told him his dad was a fireman." There could be hundreds of other reasons Billy turns into an arsonist, but only one reason is presented in the text. This is an important element of understanding inferences—we can't just infer any old thing we want; there must be evidence to support our conclusion. As the teacher makes their rounds in the classroom, this will probably be the most common reminder they will offer student discussion groups: inferences are not just made-up conclusions.

Notice that in the performance piece of this sample assignment everyone participates, and everyone, in participating, knows their piece will have an audience and even who that audience will likely be. I would give students a chance to write their stories within the walls of the classroom. For one thing, I want to know they practiced this independently more than once, and when I ask for something to happen outside the classroom, there is no way for me to know for sure who did it. I would encourage them to write several examples and then have others read them and give them feedback. As they read each other's work and discuss it, understanding would grow of how their own work measured up to their peers', another valuable learning experience. If they wanted to continue thinking about or working on this piece from home, that would be okay with me too. What if they get ChatGPT or their parent to write it? Well, they've already heard a dozen examples by now. If they can describe the task well enough that their parent or AI can understand and do it, then they really understood the assignment, so I guess I would be okay with that as long as the learning goal was achieved.

Just to refocus us, the goal is to be able to understand an inference and the textual evidence it takes to support it. There isn't a worksheet ever made that can teach like this assignment. If you think it takes too long or is too complicated, I would argue that learning anything sufficiently complicated and varied takes a bit of effort on the part of both the teacher and the student. I am willing to bet that if you look at the standards for your school around inferencing and understanding textual evidence, you've touched on many, many more in this lesson than the one I listed. This type of thinking and planning can apply to any lesson worth teaching, and if it's not worth teaching, what are we doing anyway?

Strategies and Tools for Improvement

Active Slides

Whether your school uses Google or Microsoft, you are probably already using some form of slides or presentations in your work as a teacher, but you may be looking at slides as something you make (as the teacher) and your students consume. The concept of Active Slides is about flipping the script on slides to get students creating instead of consuming information. There are many ways to use slides actively in your classroom. One easy entry point may be to take a set of slides you are using to impart information and to delete information from them. For example, if you teach history and you have a great set of slides about an era or topic, what if, instead of standing at the front and talking through the slides, you assign the slides to pairs or teams of students. Perhaps before you roll out the assignment, you delete some of the information and have students figure out how to fill it in instead of you doing all the work yourself. Perhaps on one slide, you insert a map or picture and leave a space for students to discuss what the map or picture depicts and fill in that information. Good conversations may come from trying to figure this out!

What if on another slide you leave the text and make it clear students should supply the map or image? I like this idea as a way to get started making slides and students more active because it might allow you to repurpose something you already have and also to see how your students respond to taking a more collaborative and active role in their learning. This might be a chance for you to experiment as well if you teach multiple sections of the same course. Prove to yourself that slides being more active is a good thing by trying it the way you've always done it with one period, then using Active Slides with another class. Then ask yourself which class went better? In which one were discussions better? In which class did you talk less and students talk about the subject matter more? In which was learning more rich and effective?

Perhaps if you convince yourself that making slides more active is a good thing and could improve the learning in your classroom, you will keep reading and thinking about more ways to make slides engaging and action based for students. Another thing to consider is rethinking the space on a slide as more than something you will construct and students will see. Think of them as a workspace where you can provide directions, videos, and other resources and where students can show their work or learning. One way to start viewing slides differently is to change the orientation from the default, which at this point in time is a 16:9 ratio, the same as a TV, to something like a square or orient the slide at 9:16 so that you stop seeing it as the space that fills a screen. It is a simple change, but when I do this myself, I start to think of slides in different ways that are more helpful to me.

Two different types of "Active Slides" (or docs if you prefer that format) you may want to consider are called Hyperdocs (or Hyperslides as we call them at friEdTech since we prefer to use slides) and Digital Interactive Notebooks. Both of these instructional strategies have merit as well as pitfalls. When we start recreating paper-based assignments digitally, we really have to dig in and be thoughtful about whether the assignments we are creating were effective in the first place. Without performing this critical step, we are doomed to just digitize bad practices, which makes them worse since they can be done more frequently, in a faster time frame, and they are more easily shared and spread. So it's critically important to consider in the creation process whether we are creating something that is actually helpful.

Once we've decided that there's an idea worth creating, we want to carefully consider what the student is going to do versus what the teacher is going to do. If you are creating an assignment, the main point should be the work the student is creating in order to learn, not the work you are doing in order to teach. If you find yourself getting carried away with making a cool theme or design, you might be stealing the learning you actually want to leave to your students. If you think about producing a completed assignment as the students' job, you also don't want to take away the parts of that process that might be fun, creative, and joyful, and thus, leave students with only drudgery in their work. If the Hyperslide needs a theme, what a great opportunity for a student to figure out what the theme should be and do the decorating for themselves.

In order to keep myself in check when I am designing student work, I prefer using a slide (or several) and then trying to confine my "teacher work" (directions, reference materials, etc.) to the outside of what I like to call the canvas. In Google Slides, you can choose to view the slide at a percentage that allows you to reveal what we call the "gray space." In the gray space, which is infinite, you can add materials to your heart's content while leaving the canvas a space where students are expected to produce, organize, or otherwise display their learning.

Digital Posters

There are many tools available that students can use to make digital posters. While making "real" posters gives me some good nostalgic vibes, a take-home assignment that requires resource organization is not an equitable assignment. If my

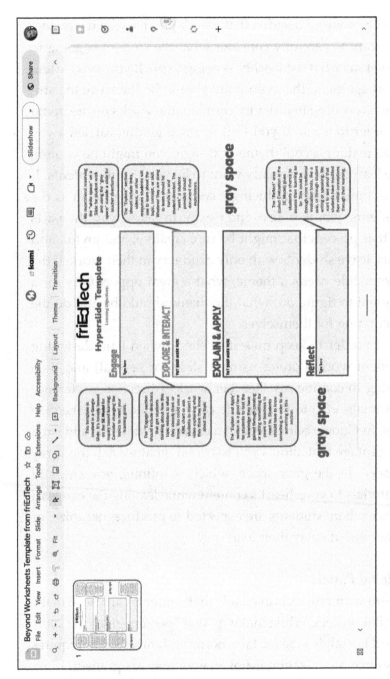

FIGURE 2.2 Grab a copy of this template at this URL: https://fried.tech/bw-hyperslide.

home environment doesn't lend itself to a 9 p.m. trip to the craft store and the ability to print out pictures from the internet at home, I have little chance of being able to successfully complete the assignment. In most classrooms today, though, this tried-and-true poster assignment can be rethought in ways that are just as helpful to the learning process, if not more so. The key to making a digital poster assignment meaningful is differentiation. Everyone should not be making a poster about the same thing but rather each student or team should be contributing knowledge through their poster to the class at large.

Let's say we are studying the scientific concept of genetics this week. As the teacher, I will create a list of each topic I want everyone to understand. Ideally, I will tell my students something intriguing about each topic and they will choose topics. Depending on the amount of material that needs to be covered, I wouldn't mind having two teams covering each topic so there is a bit of competition. My teams need to understand that it is their job to teach the rest of the class about their topic within the broader topic of genetics. Perhaps this is one of my poster starters:

Genetics and Blood Type: Am I Adopted? This poster and this team should help me understand: how is it possible my blood type matches neither my father's nor my mother's yet I am their biological child? How are blood types inherited and what can we learn from our blood type?

In order to create this poster, learners will have to really dig in and focus on blood types and how they are inherited. They will need to learn a lot and discuss a lot with each other to answer the question for themselves. Then they will also have to figure out what to include in a digital poster format so that others can understand the concepts they have uncovered. Finally, I would like my teams to create a verbal presentation they can give to their classmates so that everyone will have a chance to understand each team's findings. The structures and supports I provide my students to do this work, the teams they work in, and what questions I construct from the standards or curriculum for them to address may vary, but the idea of learning from a conceptual basis is what will remain the same. In this model, I am not offering a load of facts, then asking students to assemble those into order; I'm making a statement, then asking learners to explain how it can be so, to prove to themselves, and utimately others, what they have learned. I have found this to be a much more powerful system, and the meaningful conversations team members end up having with each other and with classmates they teach are an amazing tool for learning.

Reflection Activity

Take out your journaling activity from earlier in this chapter. Taking what you learned from this chapter, think back once again to the worksheet you chose for your journaling activity. What ideas do you have now about a better, more interesting, and more engaging assignment that could have taken the place of this worksheet? Keep in mind that there is no wrong answer here. There are a million ways to accomplish the goal of creating new and interesting ways to allow students to practice material beyond the worksheet.

Takeaways

1. The child who needs the worksheet can't do it. The child who can, doesn't need it.

2. Whether they are analog (on paper) or digital (behind glass), "worksheets" share the characteristics of being one size fits all, similar to assessments in their rigidity. They are often, in reality, used as busy work, which is work that is meant to consume time rather than produce an educational result.

3. There are many ways to get beyond worksheets that require all students to participate in meaningful ways that engage thinking. Public performance, as well as participation in team activities, activates parts of our brains that worksheets cannot.

Notes

1. https://tea.texas.gov/sites/default/files/Redes_Eng_I_Assd_Curclm.pdf

2. https://www2.cde.ca.gov/cacs/ela?c1=8%2C6%2C3&c0=2

New World, New Rules

Isn't it kind of fun when you find a statement no one will argue with? It creates a sort of starting place when there's agreement, so here goes: *the pandemic changed everything.* Here's the shocker, though: for some reason, most schools have tried to go back to exactly how things were pre-pandemic. Did they think they were great then? No, no they did not, but as we've already established, the past is the most powerful force we contend with in education (and more broadly, in our lives in general).

Plot twist of the century: it's not working! Every educator I talk to, whether online or in real life, says virtually the same things:

Student behaviors are extreme and completely out of control.

What I was doing before that I thought was working is not working anymore.

Students are consistently so far behind.

And finally . . .

I'm looking for another job; are you hiring?

None of these responses are any joke at all. The career path of a teacher has become untenable, but if we all agree that "the whole world has changed," then it shouldn't be a surprise that trying to go back to what we were doing before is now being found to be ineffective. Think about it: if the world is different, then it stands to reason that *we* have to be different as well. However, it is my finding that few systems within education have changed, and if they have, it certainly hasn't been to the benefit of the educator. It is no wonder that when we find ourselves in the same system as before, the one that was struggling to keep up as it was, we start to behave as if things were the way they were before. No more! It's time to shake things up and think about how to engage students using something that will never change: human nature.

I heard some of you groan just now when you read the word *engage*; I think I even saw a few eyerolls. I don't have to have your room bugged to see them because I, too, have been in the endless meetings where we discuss, to death, "student engagement." And yes, I know, nothing changed then, which makes us feel as if it is impossible for anything to change now. The problem was, we weren't ready. I am prepared to say that the dire few years we've faced together have made us ready for some big changes. Another statement I could add to the preceding teacher response list is "I would do anything to fix this." If you are serious about that sentiment, then let's get started with an action plan.

Taking Action toward a Solution

First, let's look at how the process might look in its current state, and then we will compare and contrast it with a new process.

Right now, the teaching and learning cycle might look something like this:

1. **Preparation:** Behind the scenes (aka: nights, weekends, conference periods, etc.), the teacher prepares the lesson and all the materials needed. They read the content (textbooks, websites, etc.) themselves and form it into something that conveys the desired content or knowledge while meeting relevant mandates or standards.

2. **Instruction:** The teacher "teaches" the content, perhaps there is a PowerPoint or Google Slides presentation connected to a lecture; there may even be some videos thrown in there. The teacher constructs salient questions to be asked of students.

3. **Proof of Understanding:** The students are then expected to do something to show they were paying attention to said content: a worksheet, discussion, or some other familiar "tried-and-true" method.

4. **Testing:** Eventually, there is an assessment of some kind to measure whether the information went in like it was supposed to. If it didn't, perhaps we try again; perhaps we move on anyway, depending on the situation.

I want to challenge us to look at the teaching and learning cycle in a new and exciting way. Something a little more like this:

1. **Preparation:** Behind the scenes, the teacher prepares the question(s) the students must be able to answer or constructs the problem students must be able to solve in order to show mastery of the content. For example: If the standard is "understand narrative structures,"

the question might be "How do you know who the narrator is in a story and how does understanding the narrator impact the story?" An earlier elementary example might be more like this: Standard: Understand responsible citizenship, Question: What are three roles of a citizen and how do people you know fulfill them?

2. **Student-Led Learning:** The students are divided into teams and each team's job is to answer the question and provide the answer (lesson) to the rest of the class. In this scenario, there may be as many standards as needed for each team to have a separate standard (ideal), or the teacher may choose to have each team work on the same standard and share content after the work is done or it could be that a couple of teams work separately on the same important standards while other teams work on different ones. With this third option, there is the benefit of competition and a little repetition that could be helpful to learning.

    (a) The teacher may take the extra step of choosing to create roles within the team, which the assigned team member must embody to earn the grade/ credit for the mini-project.

    (b) The teacher may choose to provide some base materials, but be cautious here; sometimes the learning is in the search. Don't do too much work for the teams because, under this new model, that is now their job. The last thing you want to do as a teacher is steal the learning.

3. **Expectations Are Set:** There are hard deadlines here and the work will be shown to the rest of the class

during a pre-set time period. For example, for the size question listed in the preceding text about understanding narrative structures written for 11th graders, one class period should be sufficient once students are proficient in working independently like this. (That will take some time, but I promise that it will be WELL worth it!)

4. **Students Are Teachers:** The culminating activity is when the students become the teachers and share their lessons with the rest of the class.

5. **Assessment:** If grades are required, a traditional quiz can still be offered, or the teacher can use the "Team Work without the Team Grade" template (provided in Chapter 10, or you can access it here and now at this URL https://fried.tech/bw-group-grades) for projects of sufficient size and complexity.

You may be wondering whether a model like this would even "work," that is, would students even be able to learn this way? So, here is some research to answer this question you may have. According to a study done by researchers from the University of Michigan, Michigan State University, and the University of Wisconsin, utilizing this type of "context of learning" approach benefits students of all racial and ethnic backgrounds, household income levels, and regions. Creating this environment of teamwork has been shown to benefit all students, and especially those from low-income and underrepresented groups.[1]

You don't even have to try this method to immediately know which of these ideas would be more engaging for the students as well as for the teacher. Which has more student work involved? Which will have greater student buy-in? Which will yield a deeper understanding? From where I sit now, this model of delegating the work seems incredibly obvious. It uses the built-in accountability system of presenting to peers to solve many problems teachers face daily. I bet you are sitting there thinking about whether or not you can try this in your own classroom (you can!). I would ask you to remember a few minutes ago when I bet you were saying to yourself, "Yes, I would also do ANYTHING to solve this problem." That's where I was when I tried this sort of modified Jigsaw Method of learning for the first time. (I had NO IDEA it had a name; I was sure I was the first to think of it.) For those of you still on the fence about whether this could work for you, I want to tell you about that experience, my first time trying to avoid stealing the learning from my students.

Journaling Activity

Think about the learning cycles previously described and add an entry to your journal using the following questions as a guide:

1. Reflecting on your own experiences, why do you think the first cycle is more widely used, even if the majority of educators can agree that the second cycle is more engaging and effective?

2. Think back to your own time as a student, specifically a time when the first cycle was used. How could the second cycle previously described have made the learning experience more engaging for you as a learner?

3. What fears do you have as an educator in implementing the second cycle? Don't be afraid to put your imagination to work here! Some examples that may get you started "fearing" the worst:

   (a) I'm afraid my students won't learn this way.

   (b) I'm afraid I won't know how to grade.

   (c) I'm afraid I will get fired.

   (d) I'm afraid people will think I'm a "bad" teacher if I'm not working as hard as I do now.

4. Now it's time to look back at those fears you just listed and maybe start to combat them. Think through the fear through the lens of "right now," then "but," and finally "so." For example:

   (a) Right now, I'm afraid my students won't learn this way. But, I'm also afraid my students aren't learning much now. So, I might as well try something new that might work better.

   (b) Right now, I'm afraid I won't know how to grade in a new way. But, I'm not very confident the grades I'm giving now are accurate or truly reflect the students' skills. So, I should probably try something new that might save me time and my sanity.

   (c) Right now, I'm afraid I will get fired if I try something new. But, I have been actually looking for a new job and feeling like I don't want to be here already. So, if I'm leaving the profession anyway, maybe I shouldn't worry about my job performance as much.

   (d) Right now, I'm afraid my peers and leadership might think I'm a bad or lazy teacher if I try this new way. But, I already feel like I'm not effective at my work even though I can't sustain my current pace. So, I should probably save myself and see if there are strategies that can be more effective with less time.

Solutions from Desperation

In my second year as a public school teacher, I taught French and English 2 (10th grade). In this story, I will be focusing on my "hardest" class; it was 2nd-period 10th-grade English, and let me tell you, it was awful. I had a couple of rival gang members in the class in addition to several other seriously behaviorally challenged students. I was shocked that the administration was less than no help. I wasn't even evaluated all year, and I never, not one time, even saw an administrator in the hallway where my classroom was located, which was not an obscure location. When I tried to write up a student for a curse-filled tirade that happened during class one day, I waited for a week with no response from the "higher ups." When I went to speak with the admin to ask about the office referral, she laughed so hard at the idea I had expected something to happen, that she literally cried. Can you believe that? (I'm sure some of you aren't surprised at all. . .)? I left her office while she was still laughing and that's when the reality of the situation really began to set in: there would be no external help available to me. I had to do this myself. Another time this was made clear to me is when I went to the sophomore counselor about the rival gang members. I told her that I feared someone would get seriously injured in my class, especially if I ever had to be absent, something I knew was inevitable as my daughter, Sylvie, was under three years old at the time and had constant ear infections along with whatever disease du jour was making its way around the daycare. The counselor seemed to listen, but then weeks went by and no schedule changes were made. As a side note: eventually, I was absent with my daughter, and as I expected, a fight did break out. My office aide (a student) was injured, which FINALLY caused administrators to get involved by coming into my classroom to break up that fight. Shockingly, after that, they did end up changing one of the boys' schedules. I still never saw an admin in my classroom that year because when they came in to break up the fight, I wasn't there.

Worse than any of that, though, was how little any of the students in that class seemed to care about any kind of success in school or my approval or disapproval, that is, not at all. I could not think of ONE thing that had motivated me in my school career that any of them cared about. The mistake I was making here was assuming that I was the "normal" student. By operating under the assumption that what worked for me, as a student, would work for everyone else, I was doomed to be constantly met with disappointment. Nothing in my admittedly limited repertoire of teacher tricks worked, and I felt the failure as my own. I looked for other jobs—clearly this was not for me, but there weren't any. And it was out of this desperation that I started the Panthera Project, so named because our school mascot was the panther.

I decided that the ONLY thing I had that could motivate this particular group of students was peer pressure, so I knew that I'd better use it for all it was worth! I told the kids that we were turning our classroom into a business and that the product we would be developing together was what we were supposed to learn. I let them know that I would be putting them in teams and that each person would have a specific job, along with job requirements, for which they would be responsible. They would do that job for the duration of the project, and then next time, they would be able to apply for a new position. I gave every team a question to answer and informed them of the relevant duties, timelines, and accountability checks that would be in place. At the end of the week, each team would have a turn being at the front of the room, and it would be the team's responsibility to figure out how to convey the answers they found to the rest of the class. If they failed, we all failed. I held my breath for a moment to see if they bought it. After a few seconds of silence, I realized that amazingly, and unexpectedly, no one was arguing with me. They were ALL actually listening, maybe for the first time that year. The questions they had were good, so I fanned the spark and got everyone started right away.

About three days into this new way of learning, I noticed one of the students, we'll call her Sandy, looking tearful and sitting away from her table group. I quickly went over to investigate. Sandy was a generally sad kid who would often purposefully provoke trouble for herself, so this wasn't a surprising turn of events, yet, but it would become one.

"What's wrong?" I asked.

Beginning to heave with sobs, she answered, "They, they, FIRED me!"

. . . My eyes grew large. "Why did they fire you?"

"They said I wasn't doing my work!"

I grew even more incredulous. None of them had done any work pretty much all year, and it was October. I couldn't believe it, had my stunt really worked THAT well?

"Okay, let me see what's going on," I replied, attempting to reveal nothing of my growing excitement to Sandy or her team.

In Sandy's team, there were some of the most difficult students in the class. In fact, her team included the most difficult student I had taught that year; let's call him Randall. I figured correctly that he had ended up being the spokesperson for the group when I asked the table what was up with Sandy crying in the corner.

"Miz Mayer! She wouldn't do ANYthing!" It was Randall, and he was FIRED UP. In the back of my mind, away from my facial expressions, I was ecstatic! They actually cared about something in my class for once. Every one of them was indignant. Outwardly, I remained unimpressed, while hiding my inner ecstasy. "Do you think if she works on what you need her to do independently for a couple of days she could come back and show you guys her work, that you would consider letting her back on to the team?" They agreed they would, and Sandy happily got to work alone, drying her tears, committed to her tasks.

What had just happened changed my outlook on teaching from that day forward. I guess it wouldn't be an exaggeration to say it changed my life. It seemed as if I had unlocked some sort of magic ability. I had no idea if what they would create would be great, or even good, but I knew they were learning. There was no way to know, in that moment, if they would learn from each other or just what they worked on themselves, but I knew they were at least learning something. This was so much better than anything I had tried before, and I wanted to shout it from the rooftops and tell everyone I knew! (Consider this book part of that shout.)

Having given you a glimpse of my school's culture, you probably won't be surprised when I tell you that there wasn't anyone who cared at the school to tell, and additionally, who listens to a second-year teacher and thinks they have the "big answer" everyone is looking for—but even knowing no one else in the school cared didn't dampen my excitement. I knew that I was onto something AND that it was important. Let me tell you, I've never stopped since. My colleagues at work still tease me about being the "world's best delegator," but before this experience, I just didn't know how to do that. Wow, did I learn.

The rest of that year is a blur, but after that realization, I don't recall writing another referral. Instead, I got to work figuring out how to continuously motivate the most reluctant learners I've ever known in my life to do the thing they were supposed to do in school with me, and that was to learn. It sounds so strange to say, but while nothing in that school changed for anyone else, for me, everything was different and new. I have names for some of the things I learned now and the most important one is "Student-Led Learning."

Learning Is a Student-Led Journey

If you look up *Student-Led Learning*, you will get many ideas about what it is and why it matters. However, since I didn't even have a name for what I was doing (as a reminder I was not evaluating an instructional method, I was just trying to survive), I could only iterate, observe, and iterate again. As I grew in my skills, my ability to anticipate what aspects of a project or challenge would or would not resonate with the teenagers assigned to me increased greatly.

Here are some takeaways I would have enjoyed finding had I known how to "Google" the strategy I was honing in my classroom:

- Do not give out too much information or make yourself the expert in the room.

    This puts you back in the same ineffective role you were in before. *It does not matter what you know*; it only matters what they can learn. Sometimes this takes a measure of humility on the teacher's part.

    At the time I was teaching this course, I was very proud of my hard-earned M.A. in English. I was one of the few teachers in my school to have a master's degree that was not an M.Ed. and you can bet I was very keen to be seen as a subject matter expert. I also had a largely meaningless and completely unhelpful degree in French.

    Perhaps, in some ways, the subjects where I was much less confident helped me realize that no amount of learning I had done in the past would help me teach these students.

- The "subject" you need to become an expert in is not the "subject" you're teaching, but your students and how they might be motivated to learn.

    This realization was one that I had learned nothing about in my university classes in secondary education or elsewhere. Subject matter knowledge, then, would only help me construct the questions or problems students would work on. The expertise I needed was not about literature, writing, or the French language; it was about how people learn, and at that, I was an utter novice.

- Learning happens in the journey and is not a destination to be reached.

  Taking the journey is the goal in itself. Using the traditional lesson cycle model I outlined at the beginning of this chapter, the conclusion is that learning is a place we get to.

  But in this new model, I discovered that learning is what we do, not where we arrive. Clearly, my own learning was this way and it was so for my students as well. I shape and reshape my ideas every single day. I shape and reshape my words as I am writing this book and reflecting on it. I am never arriving at a place where I am "learned." Whenever I think I might have arrived there, I need only initiate a conversation with anyone who knows anything about what I am thinking about or working on and then my ideas may be challenged all over again. I will then find that I have not arrived once again.

- My measure of quality as a teacher is growth-oriented (travel) and not destination-driven (grade or test), no matter what any entity inside or outside the classroom tells me.

  To further this metaphor, I also do not have a map for how to proceed that works for every person. If I think about a topic I'm working on learning more about, I can only guess at what's next. Perhaps I'm given a new diagnosis at the doctor's office, a new term I've never heard before. My first exposure to it happens with my physician. I write down the word. I remember what she said to me about it, and thus begins a new learning journey. I have a "need to know" that builds my interest. Next I will probably pull out my phone and Google it. (Which I have finally "learned" for the most part NOT to do with medical information because this is where I would decide within 10 minutes the diagnosis was fatal after all, and the doctor just didn't have it in her to share that intel with me, but I digress.)

After I read information on the internet, evaluating sources as I go and wondering to myself at how much misinformation is rampant in this space, I may decide I want to hear from some real people who share my diagnosis. I may turn to a place like Reddit and find a forum where others are discussing the condition. At this stage of my learning journey, I can interact with others, ask questions, and fill in gaps in my knowledge in a more personalized way. As I live with my condition, my knowledge continues to grow incrementally every day. Sometimes I may be surprised by new aspects of my diagnosis or maybe my condition unexpectedly improves; all of this information becomes a part of my nexus of knowledge and learning. I would have a hard time even recalling, after years or months, all of the interactions and experiences I have had that led me to where I am today in my learning journey, which will never truly end.

- Students are ultimately the directors of the learning journey.

Every topic I learn about in my life that will have any meaning will have a complex and completely different path for me than for any other person alive. As a teacher, I can put up signposts along the way to try and direct the learning journey, but I cannot *actually* direct the journey, nor do I want to. NOT directing the journey too much is hard at first. As a teacher who probably learned in a series of different traditional schools, you most likely believe that directing the learning journey is, to put a fine point on it, your literal job, but it's not.

If we think back to the medical diagnosis example, picture the doctor sitting with me while I process the information. She sees I am curious and concerned. She wants to help. She grabs a medical textbook and puts it in front of me. "Amy," she says, "I know you can read, so I won't read this to you, but this medical textbook has all the information that is known about this condition. If you read it, you will undoubtedly get your questions answered." (Tami, my doctor, who is very kind and knowledgeable, would never do this and she would also tell me not to Google it.) Instead, she might tell me that every diagnosis is individual to the patient. No person's trajectory matches any other person. Few people get all of the symptoms or experience all of the outcomes described in any text. Knowing everything about a condition is useless when the only person whose diagnosis matters is one's own. She will tell me about treatment options and suggest one she feels is reasonable, and then she will encourage me to try it, wait, and see if it works. If it does, my problem may be solved. If it doesn't, she will suggest another avenue, and we'll repeat the process until something happens.

I'm certainly aware that a new diagnosis is different from learning to read and make meaning from a poem, but these lessons do have a bit in common. Reading about what a poem is will not tell me what I need to know about a poem any more than Googling my diagnosis will tell me how it feels in my body or will affect me in 10 years, which is what I really want to know. Finding a poem I love that really resonates with me will tell me more about what a poem is than any analysis of a poem ever could. This is because I will be able to understand the poem with not only my intellect but also with my emotions, and this emotional connection can become my "need to know." When I get my medical diagnosis, I may feel devastated; my mind may start racing to make up horror stories that could ruin my day, week, month, year, or even my whole life. This information is so personal that every morsel of information feels like it applies to my very soul. I will probably easily remember and internalize it even when (or especially when) it is profoundly unhelpful. Understanding poetry has the opposite problem: until I experience a poem that resonates with me, nothing I hear, read, or see about what poetry is will matter to me.

We've been approaching education like it's a medical diagnosis everyone will immediately take personally and internalize, then we have been evaluating each person's ability to remember the bad news and all the accompanying facts. We may cry out, "But why do I need to know this?" and the only prescient answer may be that it will likely be on "the test." The problem is that the disease we've been describing is not one our patient has. The disease is "you should know what poetry is" and so the prescription is "read this article about poetry and complete the worksheet." But believe me when I say that this thinking is all wrong. My students didn't have the disease of needing to know what a poem was or why poetry mattered so no amount of trying to put information in front of them to help them find a cure was ever going to work. First, I had to get each of them to find a poem that touched their soul, then I might be able to get them interested in the symptoms that caused this. By the way, I did find a way to do this very thing. Turns out, poems are now called songs, and teenagers absolutely love them. They are willing to study and talk about them endlessly, but only if you let them pick the tunes that touch their souls first.

Reflection Activity

How can we, as educators, unlock this new paradigm of teaching? Take a few minutes to think back on what we covered in this chapter and how you could use the tools given to transform your classroom. What are your concerns? How can you meet those fears, head on? Who might you go to as a resource when issues arise? These are all important questions with a myriad of possible responses. I can't give you all of the answers in this book, but I can do my best to point you in the right direction, give you some resources to lean on, and help you ask the right questions.

Takeaways

1. Returning to the way things "used to be" is not possible. The sooner we accept this and move forward to how things COULD be instead, the better it will be for ourselves and our students.

2. Ironically, desperation can lead to solutions if we let it. If you will "try anything" to make it better, you will definitely "try something" to make it better, even if it's uncomfortable initially.

3. Learning is always a student-led journey; true leaders of learning don't have the answers. Rather, they focus on empowering learners instead of trying to know everything themselves; this practice expands their influence in powerful ways.

Note

1. J. Strobel and A. van Barneveld. (2009). When is PBL more effective? A meta-synthesis of meta-analyses comparing PBL to conventional classrooms. *Interdisciplinary Journal of Problem-Based Learning,* 3(1). https://doi.org/10.7771/1541-5015.1046

Systems, Teachers, Expectations, and the Worksheet

As we've established, education is about people and nothing about people is simple; yet instead of studying people in college and how people learn, we tend to learn about subjects and systems, which are much simpler than people as individuals, which is the only way any of us actually exists. But education is, nevertheless, a giant, ongoing experiment in people interacting with other people who have expectations of their behavior and are often shocked at what can occur. When we dig into human behavior and look at a person and their responses in the context of their life, needs, and wants, we often understand things that at first seem mysterious. I want to start with a story that explains what I mean about people interacting with systems; it's a story of a child I once taught. We'll call her May.

Students and Systems: May's Story

May was a high school junior (age 16 or 17) labeled as needing special education services, but was a hard worker who was compensating well for any disabilities she may have had. I don't remember the details of what her IEP (Individualized Education Program) said was required in order for her to succeed, probably because by the time I taught her, she no longer needed any of the interventions that had been devised in order to perform in line with her peers. At the time, the "big test" (the standardized one from the state) allowed students with special education services to be exempt if the committee agreed. So, May had not taken the test since she became eligible for services. Important to the context of this story is understanding that the principal of the school I was working in at the time wanted every student categorized as "special education" to be exempted in order to raise test scores, and this was no secret to any of us (and likely no surprise to many of you). At the time, this was perfectly legal and there was no cap on the number or percentage of students who could be classified "sped" then exempted from the test. He frequently told us, "Testing is a game and you've gotta play the game." (He was a former head football coach, you see.) As you can imagine, many, many students were misclassified due to this interpretation of policy. Students who had a track record of failure on that test were suddenly being entered into special education in record numbers, whether they truly needed these services or not. Legislators who are looking at how testing requirements impact behavior must take note of how these loopholes end up impacting lives, potentially forever. I fear to imagine the number of adults in the world today who believe themselves to have an intellectual disability who actually do not.

Not being subject to the test sounded like a gift, but when you are a teenager, anything that makes you different is hard to see that way. I have no doubt now, in retrospect, that many students' intellectual confidence and self-image were damaged in order to try to "raise" test scores with this exemption. I decided before May's yearly admission, review, and dismissal (ARD) that there was no academic reason May shouldn't take the test for my subject, ELA (English Language Arts), and that I would advocate for her taking it with everyone else, no modifications or accommodations necessary. My stance wasn't directed by an idea to save her self-image, but by her success in my class. May was old enough to attend her ARDs by this time, and when I walked in and made eye contact, her smile was weak. She was humiliated and looked more miserable than I had ever seen her appear. Being wrapped up in my own world and head, I hadn't thought of how this meeting would feel for her, or how damaging it might be to any student's dignity, until I saw her face.

The meeting began and I made my case that May no longer required interventions in ELA. Inwardly, I wondered if she had ever needed them. I also shared that I had no reason to think she wouldn't do well on the state test. I glanced over at her to see a face I will never forget. Never have I seen a person so excited to be told they were going to be taking a miserable state exam that everyone hates. She was exuberant, simply shining with happiness and pride. I remember telling the committee and her parent representative what a great student she was and how well she was doing in my class. She was responsible, consistently understanding, and producing work on or above grade level. She glowed with pride. May was already doing well in my class, but after that meeting, she stepped it up even more. If I could have taught 100 students like her that year, I would have signed up for 100 extra students, that's how enjoyable she was to have in my classroom.

As time neared to take "the test," May started to get nervous. She rarely asked for my attention individually unless there was some particular reason to, but she lingered after class one day. "Ms. Mayer, can I talk to you for a minute before I go?"

"Of course," I agreed, concerned something serious had happened that was bothering her. "Is everything okay, May?" I asked.

"Yeah, I guess everything is fine, but I just wanted to ask you. Do you still think I can pass the test? It all seemed fine back in the Fall when I wanted to take it with everyone else, but now I'm worried. What if I don't pass? What if I make you look bad? What if I can't really understand what everyone else does and I fail and our school doesn't get credit for me?" She was nearly in tears; it was heartbreaking to see how much she was suffering with fear and worry. After that meeting happened, unknown to May, I had a similar conversation with the principal who was determined to exempt as many students as possible from testing through Special Education. He maintained that school was a game and said, "Mayer, we have to play the game we're in, not the game we wish we were in!" (Everything was about football to that guy.) After being reamed out by him for advocating for May's exemption being removed, I worried too. What if I was wrong? I knew he would specifically go back and look at this one student's score; it wasn't like there were even a dozen kids who had been opted back IN to the test. Most likely, May was the only one because I didn't ask permission before that ARD happened. So, I had been having much the same thoughts as May. What IF she didn't pass?

I no longer remember exactly what I said to her, but I reassured her in every way I could think of that there was just no way this failure she was so afraid of could happen. She had completed all the same practice tests that everyone else had. She hadn't even been assigned to extra tutorials. She was outperforming most of the other students in her class. There was just NO WAY she wasn't ready to take that test, which was, after all, just *one* test. We talked and I know she felt better, reassured. Less than a month later, she took that test, and no surprise to me, she did very well. However, she WAS surprised; I was just relieved that I had been right!

The Classroom Bloomers

Even though I have a minor in secondary education, no one taught me about the famous research of Robert Rosenthal and Lenore Jacobsen, in which teachers were told some of their students were poised to "bloom" during that academic year. For the purpose of the study, "bloomers" were chosen at random, but teachers believed that there was testing data to back up the designation indicating some students would do particularly well in their academic and intellectual growth in the upcoming period of time. Rosenthal and Jacobsen observed that the students randomly labeled "bloomers" did significantly better academically than their peers. This effect, called the Pygmalion or Rosenthal Effect, is well known, and is attributed to a change in teacher behavior regarding expectations of students. What this means is that if I, as the teacher, believe a student will do well, the chances the student will do well explode. The inverse is probably also true. This effect, just to be clear, is not related to any facts about the students. It's related to how a teacher's behavior in relation to their students changes based on what they believe students are capable of achieving. To summarize the finding very briefly, if I (the teacher) believe a certain student or group of students possess certain capabilities, I will teach them as if they have those capabilities, and they will rise to the occasion and appear to actually have the capabilities I believe they possess. That's pretty mind-blowing information, especially for new teachers, and it shows more than anything how much the mindset of the teacher matters in education.

In John Hattie's research, which measured the effect size of different educational strategies and situations, "Teacher Estimates of Achievement," is, on the most current list to date, the third most-powerful ranked effect size. This means that it's very powerful, topped only by two factors, the first closely related to the exact measure we're talking about. The most powerful effect of all is "Collective Teacher Efficacy," which refers to the belief among a group or team of teachers that their actions can significantly and positively impact student growth. So, how does this effect work and how do you activate it within yourself as an educator? Well, to put it simply, it's a self-fulfilling prophecy. If you can convince yourself, and thus, your students, that they are capable of more than either of you originally believed, and then you act on that belief, your students may indeed be much more capable than anyone thought or than data could predict. You are probably thinking to yourself that this is another reason you are not the best teacher in the world: you have a pretty good idea of what your students are, and are not, capable of, and so do they. In fact, you or they may even believe they are less capable than they actually are. This is also a prophecy that will come true. Either way you measure it, you will probably be right, at least that's what the data tells us.

If you think they can do it, you are right. If you think they can't, you are also right.

It makes you wonder how a random student of average intelligence dropped into a Gifted and Talented program might perform differently. Due to human studies limitations, I suppose we can't "try this at home" with a set of identical twins, but I think we already know what would be likely to happen. The twin who was told they are gifted and put in a gifted program would likely far outperform the "average" twin in the "regular" program.

But what are we supposed to do with this information as educators? After all, not all students are academically gifted; are we just supposed to pretend they are? Where will that sort of madness get us? This is something that I often think about as an educator. If I don't have an evil genius principal who feeds me false data then pops out with a surprise result later on, how can I make this data useful? What, am I just supposed to pretend like every student is wildly capable? Well, as a matter of fact, yes, that would actually be really helpful. However, if you fake it, they will know, and it will all fall apart.

As May's story showed, I really did believe that she could pass, and even exceed passing, that test; and so I treated her as such. I told a committee of adults and May herself that I believed this in a formal meeting. I reiterated it to her when she asked, and I remembered it each time I evaluated her work, which reconfirmed my beliefs or gave me another opportunity to make them true by correcting and having her work again. I don't have quantifiable data to support my guess, but I would bet that I spent more time giving her feedback than I would have if I didn't believe in her so much. After all, she had shown me that my time spent grading her assignments was valued by her and would be put to use. I also held firm with the principal when he challenged my decision and accused me of negatively impacting the school, even though I secretly worried he might be proven right. How might things have been different if I had not really believed May could do it? Might my behavior have revealed my secret belief somewhere along the way? I think that it probably would have; no one is that good of an actor. I might not have spent the extra time or expended extra effort educating May either, had I not really, truly believed what I said. While I would not have voiced that opinion to her, I might have also acted differently in thousands of tiny ways that would have reinforced her belief that she was not capable. If this had been the case, that prophecy would have been fulfilled instead of the one that was.

Just to clarify, I am definitely not saying that a teacher's belief in a student can overcome any learning difficulty or that special education services are not necessary and useful for providing equity, not at all. But I do think that this story and realization has served me over the years and still serves me today in my work with adults. Even if a student needs special education services, I can find ways to assist that student to exceed expectations, and I can share that belief

Journaling Activity

Can you think of a time where you experienced a self-fulfilling prophecy? Maybe there is a time where someone believed in you beyond what you thought your capabilities were, and perhaps, their beliefs contributed to your success. Or was there perhaps a time where you didn't believe in yourself, which caused you to fail?

Take a moment to write a journal entry detailing how you felt in this situation, how your belief (or the belief of others) may have affected the outcome, and how you could use the concept of the self-fulfilling prophecy to help yourself, or others, see more success, whether that be in a career or some other aspect of life.

with my student and internalize it for myself. I don't mean I adopt the expectation that a student with a confirmed intellectual disability can grow multiple grade levels in a year, but I do mean taking the expectations we have and stretching them to their limits to create goals that maybe we are all a little inwardly scared can't be achieved.

Adults and the System

Much later in my career, I would initiate the WOW! Academy. We still provide this learning experience at my company, friEdTech, and now the acronym stands for "Without Worksheets." Originally it was "Web on Wheels" because the academy was originally designed to achieve the goal of a successful device rollout of computers in carts with wireless access points attached (before wireless access was ubiquitous inside school buildings), and yes, pun intended. We had already unsuccessfully rolled out a different computerized device that was widely hated.

As a technology department, we started with the premise that we didn't want to repeat that disaster. We believed the problem lay in human psychology. The "failure" of the technology was a classic "problem in chair not in computer" or "PICNIC" issue. (If you hear technology people refer to someone or some software problem as a "PICNIC," this is what they mean. That's right, it's such a common issue that it has a name that virtually everyone who works with machines AND people knows this term immediately.) The acronym doesn't flatter the user, but it does describe such an important phenomenon that it's universally understood among the group. Most problems "with technology" don't have to do with technology; they have to do with how humans feel about and behave with technology. That logic can be applied to any inanimate thing, just like worksheets.

To every learning experience, we bring beliefs about ourselves that impact our performance. As a child, I believed that I could conquer any worksheet, and so I did. (Well, maybe not so much the math ones after a certain point.) As an adult, I see technology the same way. If there is someone else that can figure this software or hardware out, I believe I probably can too. As a result, I don't easily give up and go away when I initially struggle with a new piece of software. I try multiple strategies as I seek to understand the way software and hardware works. I'm persistent and positive. People have said to me, "Amy, I wish I was as good at technology as you are!" but they rarely see how much time or how many tries I've put in behind the scenes. I promise that I'm no better at it than most, I've just practiced far more persistently than they have and that is at least partly because I had a positive self-fulfilling prophecy before I started. Many technology users are not persistent or confident. To see this, put an unfamiliar operating system and hardware configuration in front of them without some sort of pep talk and you will see how quickly things can fall apart. That's what we had done previously with our failed implementation. We got part of it right: we came up with an image and a name for it that would help users refer to it, but we stopped there. Big mistake!

For the next implementation within the school system, we were committed to getting it right with WOW! carts. First, we started with an application to attend a professional development offering centered around the device, the WebPC in a cart with a classroom set of devices and the wireless access point attached. The WebPC was a predecessor to the Chromebook, a simple laptop format computer with a very light operating system (Windows CE, I believe, it was called) that basically only ran a web browser and a few very light and simple pieces of software, such as a simple photo editing tool and a very lightweight word processor. The competing hardware was the familiar, old-fashioned, "computer lab" full of desktop computers attached to monitors, wired in with keyboards and the old-school beige wired mice. These labs were unpopular because they required a sign-up in advance, which meant quite a bit of planning ahead of time was needed. They also required a trip outside the classroom. That movement to "the computer lab" inherently takes away instructional time and there are many opportunities for things to go wrong in the hallway on the way there or back. Also, the transition times to a computer lab were a real drain on the most precious of all school resources, time. We knew that WebPC could help solve this problem if we could get the teachers to buy in. From today's vantage point, you may be thinking this would be easy, but at the time, no one I had ever heard of was doing this. The carts could theoretically be stored inside the classroom or at least brought there in advance of the lesson, solving all, or at least most, of the issues caused by the traditional computer lab. The wildcard was this: how would teachers react to this new software and hardware configuration? If their reaction was positive, that is, they believed they could manage the tech with students and that they wanted and needed it to provide great educational experiences beyond worksheets, the implementation held real promise. If the reaction was negative, that is, they didn't think they could manage the tech in the classroom and remained clinging to that old life raft, the worksheet, instead, there would be no saving the hardware and the millions of dollars the district had invested in it. Students would not be integrating technology any better than they currently were, which was hardly at all.

We had to figure out how to realize the usefulness and power to transform education that we knew the Web-PCs had in them to truly have a chance to get beyond worksheets. The instructional goal for the teachers was to understand that with early, free Web 2.0 tools like Animoto (video creation tool), Glogster (online poster creation tool), ToonDoo (comic strip creation tool), and Wix (website creation tool), a world of educational possibilities could open. Further, we wanted students to be creating in order to learn, instead of just listening to lectures and doing worksheets, which is still the most straightforward way to describe what was happening in most classrooms. The summer before the WOW! Academy started, I hosted a professional development opportunity during which I practiced some concepts that would become very important to the success of WOW! Academy. I had teachers work in cross-grade level, cross-curricular teams to create projects together. They took on the role of students producing work using the technology tools, both software and hardware, that their students would be producing the following school year. I still believe this is critically important. When we have teachers do "teacher work" on a completely different device using different software, it's hard for them to make the transfer to students doing student work on a different platform with a different device. (This is not because teachers are not capable, intelligent people. No one should expect this level of transference and it is not something routinely expected in other fields.) At the end of the academy, teachers presented to each other and voted on a winning team project for each cadre. So many interesting things happened! One of those was that elementary teachers were sure they didn't have a chance at winning, but tossing that concern aside, they used their standards and had such fun creating "student work." Their belief that the secondary teachers wouldn't be able to understand their standards or process was blown away when very often elementary projects were voted, nearly unanimously, as the winners.

The original academy was wildly successful. Huzzah! Teachers often would not take breaks for lunch or would not want to leave at the end of the day because they were so engrossed in their work. If the teachers were this excited about the possibilities, I could only hope that the students would take on this excitement once they got started. My mentor, work wife, and lifelong friend Jan Robin and I knew this was special, and when the need to create a teacher academy for the device rollout came around, we were ready to use everything our team had learned to make it a success from a psychological standpoint, but there was still one thing holding me back. I didn't really know if the teachers could, or rather would, do the work to implement a new way of teaching and learning back in their actual classrooms. Would they be willing to let go of the reins to the extent that would be necessary, or were they too controlling and set in their ways? I simply didn't know; there wasn't a way to know, but I knew enough to pretend that I was sure they could (again with the self-fulfilling prophecy).

In devising the original WOW! Academy, we decided to amp up the performance part of it. We had observed how much presenting to peers had motivated the cadres from the summer before and wondered if we invited administrators from the teachers' campuses and from central office we could increase that effect even more. We decided to try it even though we didn't know what would happen. During the first half day of the three-day academy, teachers didn't know this performance piece was coming, and they behaved just as you would expect. Remember, these folks APPLIED and were ACCEPTED to attend this professional development, so we had an excellent group to start with, but they didn't really know why they were there or what they were getting themselves into. They were simply and blissfully happy just to have been chosen. They listened as attentively as you would imagine, but then we dropped the bomb: on the final day of the academy, each of their campus admins and a whole group of district admins would be observing their performance presentations in an auditorium. I told them that I had no doubt that they would present amazing materials that would inform their administrators about what they had learned, and how their students would be using technology to learn during the upcoming school year. Everyone would know seamlessly what Web 2.0 tools were and how they could impact the classroom because these extraordinary teachers would show them through their sample student projects.

Depending on how many teachers you know, you may be able to anticipate the gamut of responses we got after this announcement. There were some teachers who were excited about the challenge, most of the groups felt some anxiety, and you could tell that some teachers were utterly miserable and sorry they had signed up at all. Understandably, for most of the participants, the stakes went up significantly and everything they might have ignored earlier in the day, they now sorely wished they'd paid closer attention to. As the teacher of teachers, I became like EF Hutton in the old commercials: when I spoke, everybody listened.

I would like to tell you that the first or fifth or tenth time I did one of these academies, I looked into those teachers' eyes and believed what I was saying, that is, that their presentations were going to be wildly successful and all our goals would be achieved. However, internally I always had a lot of doubt about whether it was true. During the first few groups we did this with, we had some teacher meltdowns and a handful of people who left for lunch on day two and never returned to the three-day event, but over and over and over again, hundreds of teachers rose to the occasion in completely unexpected ways. Not only did they meet the goals, again and again, they also exceeded all of our wildest expectations. Much more importantly, for the teachers who took the concepts back to their own classrooms, their students, time and time again, exceeded THEIR expectations.

Just Believe It

If just "believing they can do it" is so powerful, why can't you just "believe they can do the worksheet" and call it a day? It's an interesting question. Believing someone can do something that has no flexibility, no creativity, and no collaboration is a simple math equation. I can believe you can lift 500 pounds, but if you lack the strength and previous training to do that, my belief will not help you actually achieve it. But if I believe you can move something that weighs 500 pounds across the room, and I let you work with a team and give you access to tools to use, you can probably do it. Especially if we both believe you can, *even if* to begin with, none of us know how it can be accomplished.

Unfortunately, in the predominant American culture, we value one skill, lifting 500 pounds by oneself, over the other, moving 500 pounds from one space to another with teamwork, tools, and ingenuity. Unfortunately, success RARELY (or maybe even never) happens that way. That success of that individual mogul (Bill Gates, Oprah Winfrey, etc.) is a fallacy. In reality, that individual person did task two (500 pounds, a purpose, teamwork, and tools), not task one (500 pounds, for no reason, alone, with brute strength).

We have to get past the outdated mentality that unless you can do something by yourself for no reason at all, you lack skill, talent, practice, or training needed to be seen as "valuable." I think that the majority of us can agree that it is much MORE valuable to be able to move 500 pounds with a purpose and a team, as this shows so many more skills beyond the strength of our muscles. The old way of thinking tips its hat to the days where a single tycoon, like Vanderbilt or Carnegie, can seem to single-handedly take on one problem, triumph, and become extraordinarily wealthy, thus achieving "The American Dream." Maybe we teach one Carnegie in our career; maybe we don't, but we teach thousands of people who can work successfully in teams to solve problems that matter together. The skills are also much more valuable and useful in everyday life, and they lend themselves to learning for individual consumption.

There are those of you who are wondering how students taught this way will ultimately perform on your own version of the state standardized test, more like the equivalent of lifting the 500-pound weight alone for no reason. I have heard many teachers voice this concern: "If they are always working in groups or teams, then they have no idea how to work independently." I hear you, but I disagree and I constantly find evidence that refutes the claim that independent practice produces greater learning than collaborative learning, or that collaborative learning is not "real" learning because it doesn't last when students work independently.

I encourage you to challenge this assumption yourself in your own classroom. Create a control group for one assignment, have them work alone on the worksheet, and do the lecture. Have another group responsible for learning as a team; it's important to make sure they have all the information you do! Give them the presentation you will lecture from, for example, but don't limit their resources to that. After the work is done in both groups, give an assessment and check the results for yourself. There's no reason to wonder about things like this when you can easily prove to yourself that collaborative learning is effective. There's also no reason not to tell the students the hypothesis you're working on proving or disproving, though I would wait until the experiment was over. By the way, I would bet that you will inevitably find you have constant management problems with the independent group that you won't face with the teamwork group.

I tried an experiment like this myself with the staff of a middle school and it was quite enlightening. The "teamwork" group got the entire task done in the time allotted; meanwhile, no one completed the task at all in the independent learning group. Also, because I had determined that the independent group must work alone, I constantly had to correct their behavior, causing me a management nightmare. The group that worked collaboratively was happier, easier to manage (as in they didn't require intervention from me, their teacher, at all), and they were able to achieve all of the goals I set before them.

Strategies and Tools for Improvement: The Question Slip

Remember, the key to doing things we don't believe we can do, at least initially, requires flexibility, teamwork, and best-case scenario, a leader who believes we can do it. It's also great if the leader doesn't "help" too much. If the leader tells us every step of how to do it, we don't *really* "do it," and therefore, we don't learn that we can. A leader who is pretending to believe we can do it will often help too much and disable their learners inadvertently. If you don't really believe they can do it and are just playing pretend, take the pretending to the next level and don't help too much. Not helping too much is hard. It will be important to create a space between yourself as the leader and the struggling learners, like a process that, if respected, gives both the learner and the leader space to figure out when to ask for help, what to ask, and the leader a chance to observe the steps taken and consider how much help to offer. For the first time in this book, but not the last, I want to introduce you to the Question Slip.

When your goal is to help students learn to be more independent, and that is always your goal, the beginning of that independence can be students relying on each other instead of on the teacher or other leader. This is true for adult learners as well. Here is an example: if my English teacher marks up my essay and hands it back to me, I make every change suggested. They are the person eventually giving me a grade. I don't question their advice, I just do it. "Oh, Ms. Mayer says a comma goes there, so I'll put a comma there." Did I learn a single thing about where to place a comma? No. Can I replicate the placement of a comma in another sentence later? Also no. I learned nothing, so the teacher failed, no matter how many nights and weekends of their own time they spent giving me feedback. If the feedback was meant for me to learn, I did not; therefore, the time was wasted. Contrast this to a peer-editing assignment. The learner is paired with a similarly skilled writer. The writer thinks, "Wow, this person is no more trust-worthy than I am at this," and they're right. They will soon learn to question every edit suggested. "Should I make this change that's been suggested to me or not? How do I know? After all, this other person doesn't know a thing that I don't also know." Now the learner is in position to actually learn something through critical thinking. The same thing happens in a student-directed team.

Question Slips work like this: I, as the teacher or leader in the learning experience, give each team one fewer Question Slips than the number of members of the team. If the team has four people, the team gets three Question Slips; if it has five people, it gets four Question Slips. The purpose of this is so that the team cannot just decide to dedicate one slip per person so that they don't truly have to make decisions about when to activate the slips. When the team has a question, each member present must sign the slip, and one person from the team must bring the slip to the leader to ask the question. If the leader chooses not to answer the question, the team keeps the slip. If the leader answers, they retain the slip. Every member of the learning group knows that tomorrow, at the beginning of class, or some designated time, there will be another unlimited question time, as there is every day of the project. This time only ends when at least several minutes have passed with no questions. At that point, Free Question Time is over and teams resume work. The teacher or leader is then free to wander the room listening to teams work out problems, argue their points, or build content, as the case may be.

I learned more about my students' learning during this time than during any other time I spent as a teacher. I worried, before I tried it, that students working in teams may just gab about their weekends or love interests and get nothing done, but what I found astonished me and it still astonishes me to this day. I never, ever had this happen. I never, ever properly constructed a project that was student-directed with teams and found that teams were routinely just wasting time. What I found instead was that when they were made to be reliant on themselves and others doing something that would be on display in some form, they did not want to stop working on it. Of course, there were personal conversations, just like there is for any group of colleagues working together in any work environment, but they weren't excessive. There was pressure from many different directions to do the work, and that constant gentle but surrounding pressure worked on almost everyone I ever taught to help them learn both soft skills and gain academic ability, usually far beyond what I initially thought possible, though I never told them they were shocking me!

Behold the humble Question Slip (Figure 4.1). In the ancillary materials for this book, you can find a few different versions of the Question Slip, including a version for secondary and elementary: https://fried.tech/bw-questionslip.

Reflection Activity

I'd like you to ask yourself a question: do you prefer to work in a group or independently? Why do you think this is? Many of us in education feel as if we are islands, only seeing

FIGURE 4.1 Example
Question Slip.

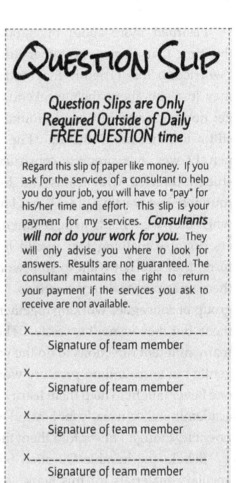

each other from distant shores, but how can we challenge
this idea and work as a community to create a better experience, not just for our students, but for ourselves as well?
Take a few minutes to think about how you can challenge
the independent norms of the school to connect, grow, and

engage with your peers in an effort to make the school experience as good as it can be for everyone.

Takeaways

1. If you believe they can do it, you're right. If you believe they can't, you're right.

2. Students can't rise to your expectations if you don't have high expectations. If you believe they can reach them, your expectations may be too low. Get a little outside of everyone's comfort zone.

3. Students can't rise to your expectations without enough autonomy to do so.

Student-Centered or Teacher-Focused

In Chapter 1, we talked about *student-centered* versus *adult-centered* schools. In that context, we were reflecting on the whole structure of the school or district. In this chapter, we are going to be focusing on the classroom itself. To be clear, I do advocate that schools return to a centered approach to management and structure; after all, if they do not, who could work there without eventually burning out? I saw a billboard recently that read "You can't put students first if you put teachers last," and I couldn't agree more. But when we move from the school structure to the classroom structure, these terms—*student-centered* and *adult-centered,* or *teacher-focused*—take on slightly different meanings.

When looking through the lens of a classroom setting, *student-centered* means that everything about the learning environment will support student learning. It is important to note that this does NOT mean that the teacher's needs are unimportant. On the contrary, I am advocating in every way possible that the teacher's time and energy be conserved and respected. In reality, every classroom operates on a continuum of student-centered to teacher-focused, but thinking through how or where different practices we put in place may land on the continuum may be helpful. For example, let's think about worksheets or, even better, packets (lots of worksheets usually stapled together). Worksheet packets fall firmly on the teacher-focused end of the continuum. As we have established, since worksheets involve no voice or choice for students and are often "busy work," they do not meet any of the criterion for student-centered learning. The only remaining reason to employ worksheets, if we understand those things, is to satisfy the wants or needs of adults working within the system mostly related to issues of management and compliance. Unfortunately, while our reptilian teacher brains tell us worksheets can help us with "management" or "compliance," this too will fail.

Let's take a look at the following table, which provides some blanket statements that are probably never 100% true but that still might provide a useful compare and contrast exercise that helps us visualize the elements of a classroom and where a real life example might fall on the continuum:

Is This Classroom Student-Centered or Teacher-Focused?	
Student-Centered	**Teacher-Focused**
The teacher's job is to construct learning experiences for students.	The teacher's job is to maintain order and convey information to students.
Students speak more than teachers.	Teachers lecture and students listen.

Students have a say in what and how to learn and in how to assess their own learning.	Teachers "cover" content and assess retention.
Students learn skills like communication and collaboration in addition to the content in the curriculum.	Teachers address social or emotional needs as behavioral issues.
Students make videos and presentations that teachers watch.	Teachers make videos and presentations that students watch.
Students are expected to keep trying until they reach mastery.	Students routinely "fail" assignments. The feedback is the final grade.
When formative assessments are given, every student responds.	Teachers "call on" students and take their answers as a representative of the class.
Students work more than teachers.	Teachers work more than students.
Students understand how the work they do leads to mastery of the objectives.	Teachers determine what work students do and do not communicate about the objectives.
Students practice more than teachers.	Teachers practice more than students. (E.g., the teacher works problems on the board/projector and students watch.)
Students learn how to think by working through complex problems and making mistakes along the way.	Teachers work through complex problems, presenting solutions to students.
Teachers encourage students to view learning as a skill they are developing with the teacher's assistance.	Teachers believe students are those who lack knowledge, which it is the student's job to master in any way they can.
Students make decisions about their learning, at times choosing the mode of learning and the products that they create.	Teachers make decisions about every aspect of the students' experience in the classroom.
Students and teachers work together to determine classroom policies and procedures.	Teachers determine classroom policies and procedures and expect students to follow them.
Students and teachers learn from each other.	Students learn from teachers.
Students work collaboratively.	Students work independently.
Students work collaboratively; when technology is implemented, one device per team is optimal when students can learn face to face.	Every student must work independently; when technology is implemented, it must be at a 1:1 ratio even if learning is face to face.
Student-owned devices may be used for learning.	Student-owned devices must be stowed during learning.

Journaling Activity

When you reflect on the preceding list citing some extreme identifiers of a student-centered or teacher-focused classroom, how would you describe your own situation? Are there times when you are more student-centered and others you are more teacher-focused? Are there perhaps good reasons why you make those choices? If so, what are they? Reflect for yourself about whether you are best balancing time and resources available to you for the best outcome for both yourself and your students. What changes can you think of that should be made? Are any resolutions for the future coming out of those reflections? If so, jot them down. Consider putting them on a sticky note on your monitor as a constant reminder. You cannot give the best to your profession if you are burned out, but at the same time, your students cannot rise to high expectations if they completely lack autonomy.

Highly effective schools foster environments that are functional for both the adults who work there and the students who attend; as a result, everyone benefits and educational outcomes are improved. A study by Lucas Education Research in 2021 found that when high-quality instruction, technology integration, and collaboration are present, a strong effect on student achievement occurs. Additionally, the research found that this combination also created improvements in behavior across student groups.[1]

Most of the time, implementing technology in a teacher-focused classroom looks like technology that is being used as an afterthought. Because, most likely, there is not a trusting relationship between the teacher and their students and the work is perceived as more like a series of ongoing assessments than a series of learning experiences, the teacher-focused classroom does not easily lend itself to technology integration in any kind of meaningful way. This is interesting because when thinking about tools like SAMR (S=Substitution, A=Augmentation, M=Modification, and R=Redefinition), we are encouraged to think of technology as a lever to use to redefine instruction. This idea has merit and technology integration and "ditching" the worksheet (or textbook, as my friend Matt Miller defines it—check out his book and blog *Ditch that Textbook*) can go hand in hand. When technology is not used to redefine or reimagine the learning environment, it shows up in other forms, for example:

Nonintegrative Ways Technology Is Used in Schools

- As a reward. . . .
  - Statement: "You can play on the computer when you are finished learning."
    - Unspoken messages students hear:
      - Technology is not for learning "'serious" subjects.
      - Tech (and other "fun" things) only have a place after the hard work of learning is finished.
      - Whatever you might learn using technology is not "real," or perhaps, not trustworthy.
      - Technology is fun, but "real" schoolwork (and therefore, real learning) is not fun.

- As a secured testing tool. . . .
  - Statement: "You can't use technology to learn because it's easy to cheat. We will use it for the test with a lockdown browser."
    - Unspoken messages students hear:
      - Teachers and other school leaders don't trust students.
      - Students will do anything to avoid "real" work even if they have to compromise their integrity.
      - What you're learning is busy work that has already been done and published on the internet, so it has little or no value.
      - Learning is supposed to be hard and/or painful.
      - The learning I'm asking of you is "cheatable," that is, low-level and not requiring connections with you personally.
- As a tool to hedge against or overcome poor instruction. . . .
  - Statement: "All students (or at-risk students) must use x program for x hours per week."
    - Unspoken messages students or teachers hear:
      - Teachers hear from school leaders: I don't trust you to adequately teach all students these skills.
      - Teachers hear from school leaders: I don't trust you to determine who would benefit from this software and who would not.
      - Students hear from classroom leaders: I did not learn this well enough, so I must prove it again.

- Students hear from classroom leaders: My teacher, principal, or other adult authority figure does not believe I know this or can do this unless the software says I can.

Statements like these tell me that educators, whether they are using or advocating for worksheets or not, have a "worksheet mindset" that I am eager to dig into and dispel. While I won't be able to say that students will never cheat with technology, I also would never say that cheating can't or doesn't happen as often using the tools of the 20th century as with the tools of the 21st century. Not using a tool for fear of a student leveraging the tool for cheating makes no sense, as a truly ingenious cheater will find new and innovative ways to cheat no matter what technology is allowed within the classroom or on the school's network.

A former colleague and current friend of mine, Dr. Cathy Moak, used to start her tech sessions with "pencil chats" where she would encourage educators to brainstorm all of the terrible things that can be done with pencils in schools. Once educators developed lists of all of the ways pencils could be misused, they would often decide, laughing, that they really shouldn't be allowed to be used at all. (I mean, if you start thinking about it, they can be used as weapons, for vandalism, to write evil manifestos, and the list goes on.) Then, it was a good time to talk about how technology *should* be used. Almost always, the educators got the point (pardon the pun); there is no perfect "tool" for learning and neither pencils nor tech are bad or dangerous on their own. Neither is designed for malice, though both can be used for such. Neither are unethical, though both can be used unethically. If your school is implementing this book as a part of your professional learning, having your own "pencil chat" might be a fun starting place.

Strategies and Tools for Improvement

Collaborative Slides

In Chapter 2, we discussed "Active Slides," and learned some ways to use tools we are probably familiar with in new ways that would be more student-centered yet educator-friendly, that is, not requiring an enormous lift on the part of teachers. Now I'd like you to consider adding a collaborative component to your use of slides. Research has shown that collaboration improves learning outcomes when compared to working on one's own. Remember the analogy about moving this 500-pound object across the room? Until we open it up to include collaboration/teamwork AND using tools, it feels impossible. The same is true for learning big, new, complicated things. To make it happen takes a proverbial village, or a learning community.

The assignment model I'm proposing here overcomes many of the barriers to implementation inherent in a collaborative assignment; however, I will remind you that learning to work collaboratively is a skill that, just like academic or other skills, is best developed over time. Even adults may struggle with working collaboratively using technology, so if you are a teacher trying collaborative work like this for the first time, set expectations accordingly. Expect there to be hurdles that, in time, will become less and less like barriers to success. Think of collaborating as a muscle needed to move that 500-pound object. The more you use the muscles, the better and stronger they get and the less that 500 pounds seems to weigh.

The content of this assignment can easily be adapted to just about any subject area or grade level, but for the description, we will envision this as a way to get to know our classmates and teacher better. I have used an activity like this to teach adults about a new software system they were implementing, and it was fun and educational for all of us. I hope you will find many, many uses for it.

First, let me give you a big-picture end-goal vision of how Collaborative Slides may look in a classroom for a student. This view should be considered for a classroom where collaborative skills have been built over time and are now routinely used and robust.

Margot receives a link via her classroom's LMS to a deck of slides. She finds her classroom number (5) in the bottom right corner of the deck, so she knows this is her slide to edit. Margot returns to the beginning of the deck to read the directions. Most of what she sees there is a review that includes the "rules" of working collaboratively in slides, for example:

1. Do not type on your teacher's directional slides.

2. Do not type on anyone else's slide OR move anything on another person's slide.

3. There is a revision history. This means that I can see everything you do, even if you erase it or type over it.

4. Use only school-appropriate words. Remember, even if you delete a word, I can still see that you typed it.

5. Be a good friend: If you are working with someone, use your digital citizenship skills to make agreements about your slide(s).

The template for this assignment is available at: https://fried.tech/bw-collaborative-slides.

Margot learns the goal of these slides is to express some aspects of her personality and that her work will be public to the class and teacher. As Margot takes a look at slide 5, which is her designated slide in the deck, she sees that she will need to answer some questions in her own words and add some pictures. She knows that she will also be able to, at any time, look at what other students in her class have done with their slides and use any new ideas she sees to iterate her own slide. There may be a component of the assignment that is done face to face and documented within the slide as well, though this is not always required, making this assignment appropriate for students who are learning remotely.

As Margot begins working on her slide, she may periodically take time to look around within the deck. If she doesn't want to be observed and doesn't need to see too closely, she can change the view of the deck to the grid view (see Figure 5.1), which will give her a sort of "bird's-eye view" of all of the work occurring within the deck. At the time of publication, the "Grid View" button (Figure 5.2) is in the bottom left corner of Google Slides.

As the teacher constructing this assignment, there are some important steps you will want to take. The first time you do an assignment like this with your classes, you will want to put students into smaller groups. Eventually, like Margot, your students will be so used to working collaboratively that they will be able to work together with the whole group, but this will take time. For the first experience, you will want to put students into pairs or triads. This type of grouping will cut down on the technical difficulties

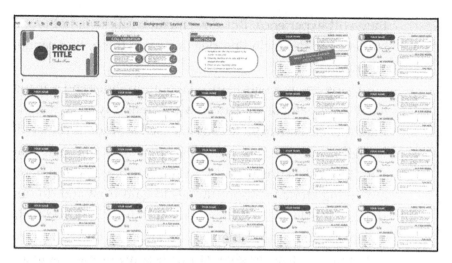

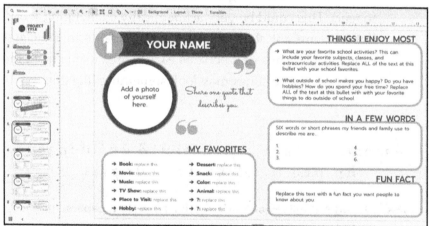

FIGURE 5.1 Grid view versus filmstrip layout.

FIGURE 5.2 Grid View button.

they will experience. But do remember, there is nothing a student can do, including deleting everything, that cannot be undone!

Using assignments like Collaborative Slides and starting small with pairs of students is a concrete way to start shifting the classroom from teacher-focused to student-centered. Assignments like this share the unspoken message that you, the instructional leader in the learning environment, are giving students opportunities to gain trust and do fun things while learning. When students have developed their collaborative muscles, they can do amazing things. Picture this: a history teacher gives students some primary sources to read. This could be very academically challenging work, but they are not alone. There are 27 students in the classroom and 9 teams of 3 persons each. Three teams have the same text, so the slides may look something like this:

America's Take on the 1918 Influenza Epidemic (High-level topic)

Teams 1, 2, and 3: Public Health Information from Newspapers. The teams are provided with three newspaper articles they will read, discuss, and disaggregate. They will document what they learn on their slides. Each team has the same articles but works in a different deck. It will be interesting to see whether they glean the same information as the other two teams that also share these articles when they observe each other's work.

Teams 4, 5, and 6: The American Military and the Flu. The teams are provided with several articles and photographs that are primary sources.

Teams 7, 8, and 9: Legacy of the 1918 Pandemic. The teams are provided with several articles and photographs that are primary sources.

There are three identical decks when this assignment begins. Each "main deck" has slides for each team within. Teams 1, 4, and 7 share main deck 1, Teams 2, 5, and 8 share main deck 2, and Teams 3, 6, and 9 share main deck 3. When this assignment is complete. There will be three main decks of slides that cover three important aspects of the 1918 flu pandemic. I would have each larger team of nine meet together to discuss their contributions to each main deck, then I would have them trade main decks with another team; for example, the teams who worked on main deck 1 would examine the work of main deck 2 and leave comments/suggestions for that team and vice versa. Each team would eventually examine all three decks, then come back together to discuss whether and how they should change their own main deck.

This assignment is infinitely more powerful than the teacher providing a lecture on the flu pandemic of 1918. Some may say a lecture is so much simpler in comparison to this assignment, and I agree. The problem is, like worksheets, it won't achieve the goal. Let's really ask ourselves what we are trying to achieve through that lecture. We want students to know that what we learn from history often repeats itself. Many lessons from the 1918 pandemic were lost to history, then history repeated itself in the COVID crisis that made itself widely known in 2020. Eventually, students will have the background knowledge to make important judgments about what could have been learned from history to prevent needless suffering in 2020 and beyond. That is powerful.

In order to do that intellectual work, most students will need a more rich and varied experience than just hearing a lecture. This is not to say that lectures don't offer some value; there are those among us who excel at learning from lectures, but even those of us who are excellent at auditory learning will not learn as much or have as deep and rich an experience as if we instead dive into original documents, read those firsthand accounts and newspaper articles, examine those photographs, and then discuss and disaggregate that information into something that we can share with others. There is just no comparison. If a lecture takes an hour and this assignment takes three hours, but with the lecture we only get 10% of the learning outcome we get from the collaborative effort, we are still better off with the collaborative effort.

If we could lecture for three hours and get the same result, that would be easier, but that's just not how learning works. The same 10% of learners would be getting knowledge out of those lectures and the 90% would still be left behind. Because we added flexibility and collaboration to the learning process, we can and will achieve so much more learning for so many more students. If we're still worried we won't be able to "cover all our objectives" in a semester if things take so much longer, we have to ask ourselves what "covering" means. If our metric is whether or not we said it aloud in the presence of students, we would be correct to assume lecturing is better. I'm not arguing that it wouldn't be more expedient for us to do so, but if we are striving for understanding and the ability to apply knowledge to new situations, there is no comparison between the lecture method and the collaborative learning approach.

Achieving and Maintaining a Centered Classroom

A truly Centered Classroom takes into account the needs of the students and their learning, but it also takes into account the needs of the teacher, or learning leader. There must always be a balance between what students need and what the educator can reasonably provide. In the previously described assignment, the teacher's lift with students who are experienced at collaborating during class periods will be to wander the room, take question slips when needed, or redirect when things are going off track. The teacher will reinforce skills and ask questions. For example, perhaps Team 2 has gone down the rabbit hole of whether COVID started in a lab in China (not part of the assignment); I would remind that team of their task and goals and that there were two other competitors in the room working with the same sources who are not falling down a rabbit hole unrelated to the assignment. This healthy competitive peer pressure is normally enough to get the conversation back to the point. If not, I would stay present with this team longer until it was back on a related topic.

During class, I would also be observing contributions. I would also likely assess student understanding separately from this assignment, which is a learning activity. For example, I might create a little quiz to sum up this assignment. I would have a high expectation that every single student would make a very high *A* after three days of rigorously reading and discussing these fairly narrow documents and topics. Then I might ask myself how these same students would do on that same quiz with that same information provided as a lecture over those same three days. I do not believe that I would have an expectation of 90–100% correct with the lecture method as I would expect with the more student-centered approach.

As far as my work as a teacher goes, constructing a six question quiz addressing these three topics and assigning it through my school's LMS is a fairly light lift. I may need a grade for the gradebook, but I do not have to take home stacks of papers, virtual or literally, to pore over all weekend to know that my students learned the material.

This assignment will not be, initially, easy to construct. Using sites like the Digital Public Library of America (http:// dp.la) can provide my topics and sources, saving me a tremendous amount of time finding sources for my students to examine and even determining topics to be examined. I have to create the main slide deck, but there is only one deck with a few slides each that is used as a template. I should not put too much work into these because they are really there for my students to build, not me. Once I have created the single deck and written instructions my students will refer to (most of my instructions are verbal in class, so these written ones will just reinforce the verbal directions), I can copy the deck three times, leaving myself with a template deck and decks for the main teams 1, 2, and 3.

Compared to trying to wrangle students into listening to me speak for several hours, this work feels like . . . less. Much less. I will have so many fewer discipline problems when students are able to talk to each other productively than I will if I attempt to "streamline" my work by lecturing. In every way, the collaborative option feels more smooth to me. And, as we discussed, if this feels overwhelming to you to start, then scale it back. Lecture one day and do a paired assignment the next day. Work your way up and up and up until an assignment like this one can make your life as a learning leader much easier than it is today. Build your teacher muscles as they are building their student collaboration muscles.

Moving from a Teacher-Focused to a Centered Classroom

If, on reflection, your classroom is more teacher-focused than student-centered, the following steps can be used to help in the transition to a truly Centered Classroom:

- **Build:** Start building assignments in ways that require increasing work from your students and decreasing work from you. For example, if you are currently building presentations that you use for lectures, begin leaving some slides blank and assigning those to your students to fill in. Continue doing the rest of your lecture if you must (maybe only during the transitionary period), but take away more and more of the content created or provided by you until your students are doing most of the content generation. If there is a slide that is "Five Takeaways from the Pandemic of 1918," leave as many blanks as you can bear and have your students work in teams to figure out what those blanks should be filled with.

- **Scaffold:** As you dismantle your podium at the center of the classroom, work on building scaffolds for students. If you begin feeling insecure that your students are not learning or if you begin to feel unimportant in your own classroom, use data to bolster your fortitude in what you are doing. (Also, please note, many students will pick up on your discomfort and actively encourage you to return to the old ways, especially older secondary students who are very used to doing as little as possible in school. If your students are resisting, this can actually be a good sign! Eventually, they will grow used to applying their brains in your classroom to do real work and will like it, but at first, you will probably hear blunt criticism. Each year when I began to change the way my high school students were learning, I heard things like, "Ms. Mayer, can't we just have a worksheet?" or "Can't you just TELL us the answers?" or "You don't do ANYthing teachers are SUPPOSED TO DO. You make us do all the work!" That last one was the *coup de grace*! I loved hearing it. To me, the STUDENTS doing "all the work" means I'm doing my job as a teacher really well. By "building scaffolds" for students, I mean providing challenging assignments students actually have to work at, but having reasonable supports to get them there. In the example here, the slide with five blanks on it is a scaffold. If you provide one of the five statements for students, that is a scaffold. Some students may need more than five or may need you to go through how you drew the conclusion to get the examples you provided from the sources; that is also scaffolding. But don't get drawn into doing all the work.

- **Assess:** Finally, don't forget that while you are using real teaching strategies to convey information instead of disguising assessments as instruction, as worksheets often do, you can still assess progress, learning, and understanding in a variety of ways. Using the methods I'm supporting here, you will have to make sure that the most quiet and reserved students in your classrooms are participating in some kind of way or at least that they are understanding. Many times if I had especially reserved students, I would have group discussions happen in discussion forums using web-based tools where even my shyest students would post. (One tool I used allowed me to create aliases for some of my students whom I made moderators. THAT was cool. I wish a tool like that existed today. If it does, please find friEdTech on social media and tell me!) I made posting/participating requirements. Once they had already offered opinions to the group in a forum online, students were much more likely to participate in small group discussions in real life.

Moving from a Student-Centered to a Centered Classroom

If your classroom is already very student-centered, but you are feeling burnt out as a teacher, you may still need to change either how you are scaffolding, how often, or when you are giving feedback to students. Ask yourself whether you can draw back scaffolding little by little so that students are becoming more self-reliant and team reliant. This is important to your mission of achieving balance for yourself and it is also better for your students' learning. Always ask yourself: "Who is doing more work here—me, or my students?" If the answer is "me," re-evaluate that assignment. Are you spending hours making the collaborative slide deck look cool? It could be that you make ONE slide of it look cool and leave the rest for your students to decorate. It won't look as good as if you do it, but that time can possibly be better spent recharging your own batteries doing whatever it is that does that for you.

The other suggestions I have, and the other area where I see teachers spending a serious amount of time outside the school day, is on feedback and assessment. There are two problems with feedback and assessment:

1. They are two different things, but we often conflate them, causing problems for ourselves.

2. They are often done in ways that do not impact learning yet are very time-consuming.

First, consider when you are "grading papers" what the purpose of the activity you're doing is for students. Here are some possibilities:

- I'm giving feedback to students who will use my work to iterate their work to the next level; I know my students are using this feedback to do the assignment again, only better.

  - If this is the case, this is a good use of time IF students are actually learning from what you're writing on their papers (real or digital) and not just clicking "accept." For example, if I say to a student writer, "This sentence does not make sense to me. Please revise before the next draft" or "I cannot find evidence of this claim in the original sources you listed; please adjust the claim or provide a source before the next check" then your time is well spent. If the update is "add comma here," it is not. If I, the learner, don't know why I'm adding a comma, I can't replicate the situation, and while I will add it, I am not learning from the advice.

- I'm "grading papers," and the marks I'm putting on the papers (real or digital) are to justify the grade to students or parents because this is the terminal version of the assignment, that is, it is not a draft, it is a summative (final) assessment.

- If this is the case, stop. I mean it; stop it right now. Make yourself a rubric. There are tons of tools or you can use any of a variety of AI tools (think Chat GPT or Gemini (formerly Bard), but there are tools specifically for teachers you can easily find that are free or low cost). If you use Google Classroom, spend the time you would have spent marking one paper and watch this YouTube video from the friEdTech channel to learn how to use the rubric tool and create one: https://fried.tech/bw-rubric-google or use a service like http://rubistar.4teachers.org/ that will allow you to create rubrics or pull down this template rubric and make it your own: https://fried.tech/bw-rubric-gdoc (replace the red text).

- Why should you "Stop it. Now."? Because with a rubric, you can provide the justification to the students and parents with much less effort. Even if you end up needing to call a couple of parents and discuss a grade, this will take much less time than providing that amount of grueling work to justify yourself on every assignment all year long. If you spend five minutes justifying each grade on an assignment and you teach 130 students, that is almost 11 HOURS. If you do this even once per nine weeks of the school year, in one school year, for one assignment per nine weeks, that is more than an entire 4-hour workweek. Stop. It. Now. Spend an hour making the rubric, then spend two minutes per assignment circling numbers as they apply. Make yourself available to meet with any student or parent who has a question; heck, you can even put that ON the rubric! Here's how that time breaks down with 130 students: 1 hour + 4 hours + (let's say you have to do two 30 minute meetings about grading—unlikely, but let's add in another hour) = 6 hours. So in about HALF the time, you have done your job, and I don't think you will have to do most of those parent meetings you're thinking you will have to. I would encourage students to meet with me about questions so that they can share their own feedback with parents. (Side note: I had ONE parent meet with me about a grade on a rubric for a huge project. When she came into my classroom, she told me, "D.D. TOLD me not to come here, Mrs. Mayer, but she always makes As on everything, so I'm sure this C is just not fair." I thought it was really funny and cool that the student had told her parent point blank she had received the grade she deserved but the parent still didn't believe it. I did something I'm not sure was exactly ethical and that I probably would not do today without the other student's name redacted, but I digress. I showed the parent another student's work, a student who had made an A. I let her look at the assignment for a few minutes, then I put D.D.'s work in front of her and asked her if she could tell the difference. She said, "I'm so sorry I wasted your time. I should have listened to D.D. on this one," and she left my classroom. I never heard from her again and she asked me not to tell D.D. she'd been there. I never did, even though we are friends to this day. D.D. is a teacher now, and if she ever reads this (her name is not D.D. nor anything like that), I wonder if she will guess it was her situation!).

Takeaways

1. All districts, schools, and classrooms operate on a continuum of student-centered to teacher-focused. Examining why, and at what point, we make the choices we do can pay off in big ways for creating a centered learning environment.

2. Taking the time to practice collaboration is valuable because this so-called "soft skill" is fundamental to student-centered learning. Ironically, allocating more time to this practice will eventually decrease the workload of the teacher.

3. There are many ways to integrate technology that are effective but only in a centered environment. The mixed messages we give through ineffective technology use are powerful and can be damaging to our district, school, and classroom cultures, both for teachers and for students.

Note

1. De Vivo, K. (2022). A new research base for rigorous project-based learning. *Kappan*. https://kappanonline.org/research-project-based-learning-de-vivo/

I'm Scared They Don't Care

When you get right down to it, one of the scariest reasons we keep doing things in the same ways they've always been done is the deep-seated fear that we teachers are actually the only ones in the equation who care: about the classroom, about the students, or about the learning process in general. Most teachers I know care deeply about both the perceived and real order and control of their classrooms. Sometimes our care for order and control can seep over into feeling like we're caring about learning, but we must do our best not to confuse the two. I've known and observed many teachers who were amazing at creating control that resulted in very little learning beyond learning to comply with some, at times, arbitrary rules. At the heart of this kind of teacher behavior is the fear and mistrust of students, parents, and often also administrators. If we keep doing what's always been done, at least there is some sort of precedent. If we try something new, we feel that we'll be entirely on our own if it goes wrong. Better to keep doing what's always been done, even if it's not effective, than to dive off what feels like a cliff. At least that's what the fear-mongering TTWWADI Monster

(That's The Way We've Always Done It) whispers in your ear. It's time to stop listening to the monster and stop making decisions for yourself, or your classroom, that are based in fear. In the famous words of Maya Angelou, "Do the best you can until you know better. Then, when you know better, do better." I love this quote because encapsulated in it is permission to also forgive yourself and move on from a "you" that perhaps did *NOT* know any better. We can only do as well as we know at the time, so let that go.

Since you're still reading this book, now is the time that you may be starting to know better, and thus, now is the time when you can also do better. How you might transition your classroom away from the TTWWADI model depends on what kind of person you are. As for me, I would just tell my students how it was as plainly as possible. I would try to help them understand what I had been doing and why, and then I would tell them what I wanted to do next and why I was going to try that. I would be completely honest about what my fears were, even if (*ESPECIALLY* if) my fear was really that they didn't care enough about their own educations and futures to participate in the learning process.

The thing is, though, this whole job of teaching means jumping off a cliff every single day. You have to trust the current process until there's a new process. Folks, this is it! It's time to accept that the "old" process is hopelessly broken and no longer working. I've heard this statement from more educators than I can count, including many who were speaking to me because they want out of the education system altogether. What we have "always done" is *just. not. working.* It's convenient and can be comforting (I guess?) to think this has something to do with COVID, but I think if we're painfully honest with ourselves, it wasn't really working before that disaster either. Maybe we're just even more tired and worn down now. Shout-out to educator Wendi Singletary who edited this book and says this: "It isn't going to get better by us sitting here complaining about roadblocks rather than moving them." You know it is a good time to change when you feel like you're hanging on to the last thread of the last rope over the last edge of the last cliff. You have to let go. There is nothing left to hang on to and little left to lose; yet that image still makes some of us (a LOT of us) clutch more tightly to the remaining threads. If we can accept that those threads were just not sturdy enough to hold us up in the first place, then they certainly are not now. Unless this is the beginning of your last year before retirement (and honestly even if it is), it's time to make a change.

I know you probably don't know me at all and have very little reason to trust me beyond getting to know me through this book, but I assure you that I trust this process of beginning to trust students. Being honest with your students is a wonderful start to the big changes that are coming to your classroom. If you think about a group of colleagues in a corporate work environment and you consider a manager whose direct reports can't stand them and who is equally suspicious and distrustful of them, you would call that a toxic work environment. I bet you would think, "I don't want to work there" and "that company will surely fail." And you're not wrong; you don't want to work there, and it WILL almost certainly fail. But we accept this sort of dynamic in the classroom. In fact, it isn't unusual at all in the educational world. But if we know it's dysfunctional, why would we do that?

Journaling Activity

Think about a time where you, or someone you know, did something because TTWWADI (That's The Way We've Always Done It), even when you, or they, knew that there was a better, albeit potentially initially more difficult, but more sustainable, solution. This could be something inside the classroom, or just something that occurred in everyday life.

Create a journal entry answering the following questions:

- Why is that the way we've always done it (tradition, rules, fear of being ostracized)?
- What did your, or their, gut say to do instead?
- Why did you, or they, listen to this gut instinct?

Sandi and Allen's Story

I had a student teacher once; let's call her Sandi. She was my former student, but unlike many of my former students, she didn't like me that much when I was her teacher. I don't think she spent a lot of time or energy actively hating my guts, but I could tell that she didn't think I was that great either. Her mom was a powerful educator, but not my variety. Let me be clear: I have deep respect for Sandi's mom; her career has been long and fruitful, but as you might know by now, I am not one to repeat the past just because that's what's always been done. I am always looking for new and better ways to do things, and Sandi, being from an extremely traditional and staid background, didn't typically appreciate my wild ideas. BUT, something must have gone well for her because when it came time for her to do her student teaching, I was one of the two teachers she chose. The other one was extremely traditional, and luckily for me, she had already done that tour of duty before she came to me. It hadn't gone particularly well, which set her up to, perhaps, think I might know a few things she hadn't realized before.

I had to ask her why she picked me, her former Dual Credit high school/college English teacher who we both knew she didn't love. She told me that her first university English class was a sophomore-level class she qualified for because she'd taken both freshman courses with me during high school. There, she realized that even though she was a very fresh freshman, she actually knew much more than she realized she had learned. She had to grudgingly admit that I must have been a pretty decent teacher because no one else in the class was as prepared as she was. This pleased me to no end, but I did wonder how our teaching styles and educational philosophies were ever going to align for a successful student-teaching experience.

As Sandi settled into her student teaching, she realized we had five difficult classes and then one VERY difficult class. That class was so memorable that we gave it a nickname: "Third Period." To this day, we know exactly what we mean by that. This class was one of those that could drive you to call in sick or even leave the profession. I'm not sure Sandi had ever even been IN a class like this one as a student (on-level, special education inclusion), much less tried to manage and teach it. It was daunting for me, and I was a pretty experienced teacher by this time. After a couple of weeks, I understood her university's student teaching model that was supposed to ultimately lead to her teaching the class without me even in the room. She, of course, knew this from the beginning and had been worrying about it all along. One day, in particular, Sandi made significant eye contact with me and said, "Ms. Mayer, *please* don't leave me alone with 'Third Period'!" I told her I wouldn't, then immediately, within the next two weeks, broke my word when I got food poisoning. As a result, she was, indeed, alone with "them" for nearly a week. I'm sure it was no fun at all.

Once I returned to school, though, she and I had a pivotal discussion. I don't know if she remembers it, but it's one I will never forget. I had told her how hard it was to be a good teacher to a kid you didn't like and that I felt like it was part of my job, a serious duty, to find something to like about every "kid" who was assigned to me. It wasn't always easy and sometimes it actually seemed impossible, but I did keep trying, scouring their writing or their person for some humanity I could appreciate. Sandi had a particularly rough time with a student we'll call Allen. She said to me, "Ms. Mayer, I can tell you actually *LIKE* Allen. But I don't get it. I can't find a single thing to like about that kid. He drives me crazy. I wake up every day hoping he'll stay home, but of course, he's ALWAYS at school. I just cannot stand him." I chuckled at her honesty. It was good that enough barriers had come down between us that she could share this with me because I figured I could actually help solve this problem.

In my classroom, every day began with some sort of writing assignment in a composition book. Daily writing is a topic I'm extremely passionate about and one of the strategies I use as an English teacher and that has paid off the most richly of any that I ever implemented. As you'll see in this story, it paid off in more ways than just improving student writing. I recommended to Sandi that she grab Allen's composition book and just spend some time reading it until she found something, no matter how small, that she could connect with or could possibly like about him.

In contrast to Sandi, I knew a lot about Allen already. I'd read his composition book and spoken to his Dad. It actually didn't occur to me why I liked the kid when I was observing all the same behaviors she was. Sandi cleared that up for both of us and it only took her about five minutes. I saw her put his composition book back on the shelf almost as soon as she'd taken it down. "Well," I started, "that didn't take long. Did you already find something that made you change your mind about him?"

"I did, and it was on the very first page I read. I've just been staring at it this whole time. It was his 'I Wish' poem." In an "I Wish" poem, every line starts with "I wish." "The first line of Allen's poem was "I wish my Mom weren't dying of cancer right now. And I'll tell you, Ms. Mayer, it wasn't a lot happier after that. He's got so much going on right now for a 16-year-old. No wonder he's always looking for a good time and a laugh. I had no idea his life at home was like that."

If I remember correctly, this was the last conversation Sandi and I had about Allen or his behavior. He never knew that she'd read his "I Wish" poem or that she'd learned about his mom's cancer diagnosis. His behavior probably didn't change one bit, but what did change from that day on was Sandi's entire energy toward Allen and I never remember another battle of wills or issue between the two of them. I don't think we were suddenly letting him get away with anything; I just think that the quality of the relationship changes when the stories that create the animosity fall away. Sandi had been telling herself a false story that Allen was trying to "get her goat," that his objectionable (to her) behaviors had something to do with her, and so they felt personal. She didn't know any better, so there was no way that she could do any better. Meanwhile, in reality, Allen was just being himself and maybe a little more reckless than normal because of the incredible stress he was under. None of his behaviors, whether we deemed them good or bad, had a thing to do with me or with Sandi. Once she realized that, the tension quickly drained out of the relationship. It felt like when you're playing tug of war, and the other team suddenly gives up without warning. If there's nothing to pull against, there's no sense in trying to keep on pulling. In fact, you can't do it.

Trust Fall

By this time in my career, I had learned to trust the process. I realized that if I could allow myself to get to know the people I was responsible for teaching that I would figure out what made them care and that I could help them care about their education and their future or at least what I thought was best for them to get them to do the things necessary to help themselves. It did feel like jumping off a cliff without a hang glider at first, but with nothing but one, small, frayed rope to hang onto anyway, I figured I might as well give hang gliding a go. It worked. Every time, year after year, tough kid after tough kid. It works today with the tough adults I now encounter in professional development situations too. If I can understand you and find something to relate to within you, then I can teach you something new that will help you; if not, I don't give us good odds.

This is one of the many reasons why I believe in asking every student to respond to: "Tell me about the best or worst experience you ever had in _____" (fill in the subject you are teaching). For me, this statement was "Tell me about the best or worst experience you ever had in English class." I asked it of every student, every year, no matter the age, and it helped me so much to understand what I started thinking of as the invisible baggage every student hauls with them to school every day of their lives. Sometimes the luggage they bring helps them gain confidence and be successful, and a lot of times, it explains why they come to school on the very first day feeling defeated and seeming burnt out. I strongly recommend, no matter what subject or grade you teach, 3rd grade or college, if your students can write or speak (this assignment could be done using Flip, Screencastify, or any number of video tools as well) that you ask them to write or talk for 10 whole minutes about this subject. I prefer it in writing for those who can do it, but it's the information that's important, not the medium.

I remember a child I'll call James, who came straight into my classroom as a junior and put his head down after only about two seconds of eye contact on the very first day of school. I had to wake him up (could he really have gone to sleep that fast?) to start class. He might have been the first student that year I gave my "fried English" speech to. I told him, "James, I can see you're not very excited to be here, but let me tell you something, this is not regular English class, this English class is fried!" That statement always evoked a puzzled look. "You know how when you go to the fair all the food is fried and it's so good? You will try eating just about anything they have there because it's fried, so how could you go wrong?" I might have seen a slight nod. "Well, that's how this class is. Yes, it's English, I'll give you that, but we're going to fry it up so it won't taste so bad." I smiled and he looked suspicious. But, then we started class, and I asked the "best / worst experience ever" question. It was no surprise that I got a suitcase full of bad experiences from James.

I obviously ended up seeing many other teachers' names over the years and hearing many horror stories from my students about them. Let me just tell you, I doubt any of them would have been told the same way by the adults in the situation. For example, James really believed that in 3rd grade, his teacher told him that he was a terrible writer and should basically just stop trying. I am fairly certain that no one ever said that to him, but even as a world-weary 16-year-old, he still sincerely believed that's what happened. Irony of ironies, he was a good enough writer to convey all of the indignities of his younger self within the 10 minutes of allotted time and in a compelling enough way that I remember his ire all these years later. I don't recommend arguing with kids about what they think happened. What they THINK happened is what they've got in that suitcase; their perceptions are their realities. All we can do later is help them unpack those suitcases and put new and better things in there. Once James knew that I understood his story and once I assured him that his writing was, in my expert opinion, on or above grade level, perfectly comprehensible, and so on, he did a lot more sitting up and paying attention in class and participated in just about everything I asked him to do, especially if it had to do with writing.

My point is, on the very first day of school that year, James had already decided that he was shutting down the jets in English class. I don't know how he acted or what he did in his math class that day, but it could have been quite similar. Once I showed him that I cared and took the effort to understand his experience, everything changed between us, just like it did between Sandi and Allen. This strategy costs nothing to implement and is zero risk. If you're afraid your students don't care, this is an excellent place to start proving to yourself that they do. I hope you'll try it!

Reflection Activity

Think back to our journaling activity earlier in this chapter. After reading the case study presented, think about how you, or your friend, may have done things differently by following your gut instead of following the TTWWADI monster. Try putting on your best optimist hat and think what could have happened if this resulted in wild success.

- How might those who were affected by the decision have interacted with you differently?

- How can you lean into trusting that gut in the future, rather than caving to the TTWWADI monster?

- Why are we all so afraid of moving away from norms that we know are not good enough for us and our students?

Digital Interactive Notebook Activity

Digital Interactive Notebooks (DINBs) are familiar to most teachers today, especially if you remove the word *digital* from the title. The purpose of the notebook is to become a place where students practice skills that are highly personalized to each student. However, as the teacher, it can be hard not to do too much of the work and turn the activity into a digital worksheet. When you're creating DINB pages or assignments, you should always ask yourself these important questions:

- Who is doing more work and spending more time on this assignment: me, or an individual student?

- Am I doing the "fun part" and leaving the drudgery to my students? For example, there are so many beautiful interactive slides that have been published on Twitter and Teachers Pay Teachers, but as a student, the decor may either not matter at all to me or be something I would learn from doing myself.

- Finally, is the skill practiced here worth the time and effort to put the assignment together? If I spend three hours creating an activity that could have been easily practiced on a blank digital file or piece of paper in 30 minutes, that is not a good, centered use of my time.

There are some good, flexible DINB pages that can be created and reused countless times. In the language arts classroom, for example, I might use something like this story structure page many times throughout the school year to allow students to map out increasingly more complex story structures:

Beginner DINB example: this plot diagram (Figure 6.1) has the pieces of the story structure in place; all students need to do is double click in the box to add their description. Thus, this page serves two purposes: to teach that stories follow a similar arch and to apply that knowledge with a particular story the student has read. This could be done with a film or even an episode of a TV show as well.

Intermediate DINB example: With the DINB page shown in Figure 6.2, students would need to know, remember, or look up how the elements of plot go together. There is less

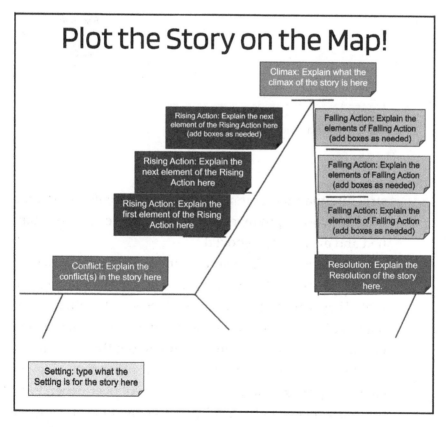

FIGURE 6.1 Beginner DINB plot diagram.

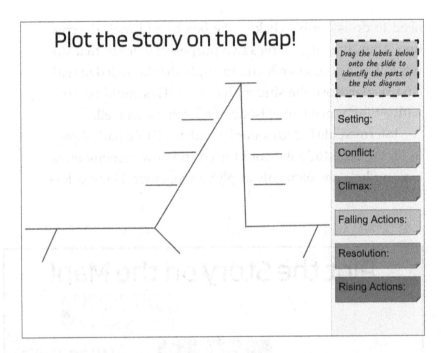

FIGURE 6.2 Intermediate DINB plot diagram.

structure than the example above. As students grow more used to working independently, scaffolds can be dismantled and eventually removed.

Advanced DINB example: In the version shown in Figure 6.3, students would need to know the parts of the plot. They will be providing the labels, determining how many points of rising or falling action there are, and where on the diagram it would make sense to put the elements.

It's a good time to think about how using technology to complete practice can be an improvement over paper. With this particular example, aside from saving time and energy in the copy room, students can make it their own; it's easy

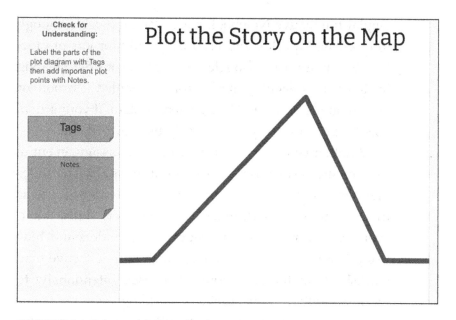

FIGURE 6.3 Advanced DINB plot diagram.

to extend the assignment as well. For example, "When you finish your plot diagram, create a color scheme that corresponds to the mood of the story or add three pictures that you would include in an illustrated version of this story."

When you are creating Digital Interactive Notebook pages for your classroom, it is a good sign if you can think through how the first version of the page may look in comparison to the third version. What scaffolds will you initially provide? In what order will the elements be taken away most logically? Will there be students who require modifications? If so, what elements of the scaffold may remain longer for students who need more time or practice to internalize what they are learning? As you reconsider how students will practice in your classroom, assignments like

Digital Interactive Notebook pages can be flexible enough to be created quickly and used frequently for lots of practice. If you are using Google Workspace, consider creating in slides and assigning them through Google Classroom or your school's Learning Management System. If your school uses Microsoft tools, you will likely use PowerPoint.

Another consideration is that you may assign an entire deck of slides corresponding to a unit of study. The slides may remain blank or have guidelines students will use as they encounter opportunities to practice new skills. Whatever the case may be, it is important to understand how using DINBs in this way can be much more effective than worksheets in the classroom when used intentionally to reinforce skills with decreasing scaffolding.

It's also interesting to note that the more advanced students' skills become, the less work the teacher is doing. This increasing competency of students leaves more time for working with those who need more interaction with the teacher and more scaffolding. It's another win-win for a centered classroom.

Takeaways

1. Change is scary! However, when we examine what we're hanging onto carefully, it is likely even more frightening. Letting go can, and should, be freeing.

2. The stories we make up in our minds about why people do what they do and how that relates to us creates friction. Conversely, understanding people and their

motivations helps us understand them in new ways that are instantaneously healing.

3. Creating scaffolded assignments that we can use modified versions of over and over throughout every school year is a powerful practice. Especially if we create them thoughtfully and change them subtly as our students' skills grow, leading to a release of control and a clear proof of learning.

Behavior, Motivation, and the Worksheet

Consider these three elements: student behavior, motivation, and worksheets. Initially, these three things seem disconnected, but they are, in fact, pretty intimately related. Worksheets are created with an inherent disconnection from context, differentiation, and relationships, all the things that make education real, useful, and fun, both for the teachers and for the students. Not once has a grownup ever stopped me in the grocery store to ask if I remembered a worksheet they did when I was their teacher, but plenty asked me if I remembered their research (or other) project. That is, after I really learned how to create a research project that mattered. In this chapter, we're going to try to understand why worksheets are so profoundly unimpactful and unpack some alternatives. The research project I'm referring to here is just an example, one that may or may not apply to your grade level and subject area, so please let it stand in for something that works for you. Before that time, I don't remember one single unique thing about any individual student's work. I remember index cards, citations, and endlessly trying to explain, in vain, why all that was necessary.

I don't remember any of these details for one simple reason: there was nothing individualized or even important about it. Even so, the task of individualizing assignments or making them "important" feels daunting when you are currently living in a worksheet world. (Even if you are not actively using worksheets on a daily basis, the word "worksheet" is a mindset that represents a way of doing schoolwork beyond the literal document here, so you can be living in a "worksheet mindset" with or without a Teachers Pay Teachers account.) In this chapter, I want you to think about the suggestions to pivot assignments to larger views with more interesting and important implications. The examples given are not meant to necessarily be literally implemented in your classroom, but rather to help you understand the concept of taking something that is "worksheet mindset" and pivoting it to "beyond a worksheet."

If I think about the work my students did after I understood how to teach research in a meaningful way, I start to remember so many projects! I remember Nathan's paper dolls, which showed the complexity and beauty of clothing in Shakespeare's time that so fascinated him. I remember Sara's work explaining the connection between math and the beauty of a human face, especially how she examined the symmetry of the most popular kids in their grade and how shockingly symmetrical each of their faces were. I remember when Ashley studied design and decor and redecorated her room in real life, or when José and his dad built a kit car together, and he researched and documented the process from start to finish.

Not only do I remember all those projects, and more, I also remember how excited students were to work on these projects both inside and outside of the classroom. I remember how they didn't want to stop when the bell rang, and how they kept working on them at night and on weekends and wanted to talk about them for months after they had been turned in, or even in the grocery store more recently. I remember how little the grades seemed to matter to them and how the work became the important thing, not just checking a box required by the state. I remember weeks of not having to correct anybody's behavior because almost everyone was on task doing something they cared about, wanted to work on, and believed was important almost all of the time. I can easily compare and contrast that feeling with the one I had back when we were slogging through notecards, which was like pulling teeth out of live and squirming victims. Notecards with research notes may not literally be a worksheet, but they have the same vibe and they work just as well at sucking the life out of a classroom.

Once I figured out research didn't have to be what I was making it the first year, I tried to teach the skill of "writing a research paper." I kicked off research projects by explaining the project trajectory. (Please remember, even though I'm going to explain this process in the context of a research paper, these same ideas and concepts can and will work in any subject area; mine just happens to be English.) Anyway, the idea was that everybody would write a research paper, but the goal was to pick a topic that was so fascinating that they found it irresistible. They would write the paper themselves, but then after all the papers are written, each student's job would be to sell their research paper to their team that can only pick one topic to pursue. After that, the whole team would work on the chosen researcher's topic.

The idea was not even to pick something you thought other people would want to work on, but to pick a topic that was so fascinating to *YOU* that YOU would want to work on it. If other people happened to agree, that would be *lagniappe* (something you get that is extra, and great, yet unplanned).

Some students knew exactly what they wanted to pursue from the get-go, but more commonly, it took a bit of discussion with me to get there as far as topics went. We tried not to hurry this part, but as more and more students settled on questions they wanted to answer, the urgency for everyone who was still undecided ramped up. I remember talking to one student, we will call her Jenny, about her topic. She'd seen a *Sally Jessy Raphael Show* (in case you don't remember, she was a 1980s talk show host with short blonde hair and signature red glasses, like budget Oprah, but with less class) about a medical condition that was little known at the time called intersex. The people featured on the show had mixed sex characteristics or chromosomes that made Jenny think about gender in a way that she hadn't before. She was fascinated and couldn't wait to dig in to learn more. I was intrigued too, and as soon as we had this conversation, I started seeing and hearing about this condition everywhere (isn't it crazy how that happens?). I was able to contribute by recording for her a documentary I saw coming up on the Discovery Channel.

One of the experts on the subject that had been on the talk show was Dr. Tiger Devore, not only an expert on the subject, but also an intersex person who was assigned female at birth. Jenny had been particularly interested in him, which gave me a potentially wild idea. Why not have her call his office and see if she could interview him? I would have thought there were maybe 100 things standing in the way of this working, but within a few days, Jenny was in my classroom during lunchtime doing just that! I can't say I didn't cringe at some of the questions she asked Dr. Devore, but thankfully he was kind, patient, and took a great deal of time making sure she understood his responses. I couldn't believe it: one of my students had just interviewed a world expert on a complex subject none of us knew anything about only a week or so before; it was astounding. I was so proud of her and was just as impressed with him. The doctor even agreed to answer emails from her should she need more help during the rest of her process. I've since seen Dr. Devore on TV a dozen times, and I have such a warm place in my teacher's heart for the time he took for my student.

Ultimately, Jenny's team ended up choosing her research project to turn into a presentation for not only their class, but also the administrators from our campus and a few from our district's central office as well as the rising sophomores who were considering taking Dual Credit English, the class that Jenny was taking when she did this project. I was a little nervous that such a sensitive subject might not get the respect Jenny, and by this time, her teammates should have earned through their diligent, scientific and medical work. But, to my immense pride, they pulled it off. There was not a giggle or a snicker as they educated a packed classroom about the medical condition, how medical professionals responded to the condition in the past versus at that time, and how intersex people themselves wanted to be, and deserved to be, treated. I would be completely shocked if every student and educator in that room doesn't remember that presentation and the professionalism the students who gave it displayed; I'm still impressed all these years later.

Journaling Activity

Have you ever done, or had a student do, a project like this—one that you remember years later and will likely never forget? Spend some time thinking and writing about what made that project so special. What extra steps did you, or the student, take to make the project stand out so clearly in your memory? Did it have cultural significance, ask hard questions, or did you or the student just have a particular passion for the topic? Whatever the case may be, think about what made the project so memorable and how you might be able replicate that experience for students in the future.

This Work versus that Work: What's the Big Difference?

If you can, compare and contrast what these students accomplished with how things might have been different with a worksheet or packet. Once again, the context (in this case, the topic and the connections to other people) changed everything. I'll warrant that none of the students in this particular English class would have had behavioral challenges no matter what content was provided to them. However, the same result was achieved with the students in on-level English, a sizable percentage of whom had significant behavioral problems in other classes, even being gone for weeks at a time in alternative disciplinary placements. I rarely knew what they'd done or in which class or hallway the infractions had occurred, but I also couldn't imagine most of the students who were suffering those punishments doing anything "bad" at all because, in my own classroom, I just didn't see those behaviors unless I got off track with my instruction, in which case, the behaviors helped drive me back to the path of engagement quickly. You can use unwanted student behavior to tell you about your instruction just like you use formative assessment to tell you about student learning.

And after doing some additional research, lo and behold, the experts agree. According to a study in 2021 conducted by the National Center for Learning Disabilities,

> By integrating behavior supports (e.g., instructional choice, preteaching, opportunity to respond) into our instruction, we strengthen proactive behaviors and reduce the probability that challenging behaviors will occur. That makes it less likely that we'll need to rely on rewards or consequences to encourage positive behavior.[1]

As we consider student motivation, it might make the most sense to examine what motivates and demotivates us within our school and work environments. Even the words, sometimes especially the words, we hear can change our emotions and motivations. This should make total sense in the social media driven world we live in today. Consider the "would you rather" scenarios in the following table and examine your own reactions to the wording:

Would You Rather . . .	Or Would You Rather . . .
Attend a Whole Staff Mandatory Training	Choose the Break Out Session You Want to Attend
Get Assigned to a Predetermined Committee	Opt in to a Movement that Excites You
Start a New District-Created Procedure Wednesday	Choose Whether You Start in the Early, Middle, or Last Implementation Team

Would You Rather . . .	Or Would You Rather . . .
Have a Task Delegated to You	Create a Solution to a Problem that Helps Everyone
Be Assigned to Attend Standard Summer PD	Apply to be a Part of a Special Summer PD Program

What's on the left side of this chart versus the right might, in reality, be exactly the same thing, but how they are different in concept is very important. It's strange that we think our students will react any differently from ourselves to the context we give them for the work they do. All we have to do is think about how we want to be treated and what would motivate us to be happy and successful, how we wish and hope things would be, and then create that situation for our own students in the classroom whenever we can. Ironically, many schools have become so deleterious to adult mental health that educators are showing up desperate for relief; this is a difficult and perhaps even impossible situation from which to create the kind of changes that would make schools fun places to be and learn within.

Creating Motivation Out of Nothing at All

I know that it sounds like I'm suggesting we have to be highly entertaining every day in school, but I really do not mean that; it's impractical and, even worse, likely impossible. I mean that there are elements of student work that make it connect to students' hopes and dreams, and sometimes even fears, in ways that are very motivating. You experience this all the time yourself. For example, when you watch HGTV or YouTube videos about doing something that you're thinking about doing yourself, something connects in whatever way to yourself. Here are some practical ideas for how to increase buy-in when you're creating an assignment:

- Think bigger: if you are only looking at one standard or skill, try to think about how you can expand that concept and connect it to a larger set of skills that will lend themselves to a bigger picture, for example:

Initial Skill	Larger Set of Skills	Suggested Student Output/ Performance Task
Subject/Verb Agreement	Writing with Correct Grammar	Create, produce, and publish a social media post, article, or YouTube video that ethically achieves your goal of views, likes, etc., for an audience that requires careful and correct language usage.
Area Formulas for Shapes (parallelograms, trapezoids, and triangles)	Decompose Shapes to Find Area	Create a plan for a house you want to live in using at least two unusually shaped rooms and get your class to vote your design the house of the year.
Compare the Cultures of American Indians Prior to European Colonization	Understand How Culture Is Changed by Human Migration	Create a presentation, book, video, or other product exploring the culture of a tribe of native peoples for a specific audience. (Be sure to define the audience: it can be another teacher's class, invited guests, school administrators, etc., based on your goals and availability. Remember, the audience can also be virtual, either live or recorded, but they must be a REAL audience.) Teach your intended audience what they need to know about your chosen group and make sure they know how your group is alike or different from other contemporary groups and how your group changed and remained the same after colonization.

Initial Skill	Larger Set of Skills	Suggested Student Output/ Performance Task
Understand Scientific Investigation	Apply Scientific Investigation Strategies and Techniques to a Local Issue	Create a persuasive presentation for local leaders regarding a community problem; provide scientifically collected evidence to prove your points then present to the local leadership. (This could be a school problem—mold in the ducts? Poor nutritional value in the cafeteria food, etc., or a wider problem like pollution in the watershed?)

- Consider the audience for the work: whenever possible, your audience should include those from outside the immediate learning community (the classroom). Trust me when I say that this will naturally encourage the students' excitement level to go WAY up!

- Consider whether the work being done could help someone, or at least, educate someone outside of the classroom: for example, do 3rd graders know this? Do they need to? Can your students teach them?

  - Sometimes helping someone else is SO powerful, you might use it to create a motivational system in your classroom that is not necessarily connected directly to the standards.

    - Example: I worked with a 6th-grade teacher on a "Reading Project" during which her students were paired with 2nd-grade students. Each week, the 6th graders worked on learning to read aloud and with feeling a particular children's book. On Thursday and Friday, students connected via a video chat tool with the individual student they had been assigned to read to. They read the book to the younger child, asked them questions along the way, and discussed the book with them.

This project turned out to be so motivational for both sets of students that the teachers noticed a near lack of any behavior problems in their classrooms. The 6th graders were required to maintain a certain average to continue participating; one student of particular concern before the project started doing daily work for the first time. When questioned about the change, she said she was worried if she didn't do her work, her assigned 2nd grader might be the only one who didn't get the story that week. Her teacher was amazed and gratified because before this project, she would have said the student was impossible to motivate.

- Try to find a way the work can be applied or connected to the "real world."

  - Example: I had a student whose mother worked for the local Lions Club (a charitable organization). The organization needed to have a website created, but had little funding and no knowledge of how to make that happen. Our class decided we would take on building the website for them in exchange for a $250 donation to our classroom fund. Students interviewed the Lions Club members, drafted and edited written content for the site, figured out how to get the domain hosted, and produced the website in short order. We all learned so much from the experience that there was no end to the standards for reading, writing, listening, and speaking that could be connected. Plus, we helped a local organization and didn't have to ration school supplies for the rest of the year.

- Another example is just interviewing folks in the community outside of the classroom about things happening inside the classroom. For example, one year I was wondering to myself why we still had every student read an excerpt from *Beowulf*. Yes, it's a famous and ancient piece of literature, but what was the significance or did it have any at all? (Worst-case scenario, and my secret fear: we only read it because of the TTWWADI.) I assigned my students to go out into the community and interview people to find out and report back to me and the rest of the class. What happened as a result was completely unexpected, probably even more so to me than to my students. What we learned was that men, especially, remembered and were enthusiastic about *Beowulf*. It had been one of the few pieces of writing they had enjoyed during their own high school English careers. I was prepared to scrap it (in my state, the standards don't include specific works of literature), but the students *insisted* we read and study it because it was "so important" to many of the members of their community that they looked up to. Instead of me trying to "make" them read and understand it, the tables were turned. It was them convincing me that this was important work, which felt much better to all of us.

- Figure out how to truly empower students instead of just delegating the work.

    This part can be hard because empowerment and delegation are different, but unless you are the recipient, the changes seem subtle. When I give you a worksheet, it's implied I already know all the answers and that you should all come to exactly the same conclusion I have; this is delegation 101. At work, it looks like I am assigning you a task that I actually already know how to do but don't have time for or that is beneath my station. For example, alphabetize these files; we both know what needs to be done, but since you're lower on the org chart, that job becomes yours instead of mine. This is a clear example of delegation. It doesn't feel great to the person being delegated to, and it feels even worse when the "job" does not need to be done and helps no one. For example, alphabetizing these cards that we're planning to throw into the trash tomorrow feels much worse than alphabetizing these cards so that later we can actually find the card we need when we need it.

Empowerment, by contrast, means we are working to solve a problem that neither of us necessarily knows how to solve. This can be scary when you're the teacher and you have been taught that the teacher is always in charge of not only what is to be learned but also exactly how that learning is supposed to happen, not to mention our societally ingrained need to have all of the answers. To empower someone, I have to trust that the student can and will figure it out, and I have to get out of the way for them to do that. When we took on the Lions Club project, none of us knew for sure how to do the work or even what work there was to be done. I had to trust that my students would rise to the occasion, care about the work, AND that they would actually complete it. I couldn't just delegate it because I didn't know what the work even was, and if I had taken that over, I would have ruined the experience for them. (I would have

STOLEN the learning opportunity from them.) It only worked because I did a lot of shoulder shrugging and saying "I don't know" when they had questions. Saying "I don't know" is actually a power move all teachers should be more aware of. Now that there are a thousand ways to find something out that we don't know, there is no reason for teachers to even pretend to know something when they do not. It's a much more powerful position to admit (or even pretend) you don't know the answer, and then work with your students to figure those answers out together.

- Use collaboration whenever possible.
  - One of the things I realized when I had my initial lightbulb moment was that the students whose behavior was the most concerning to me did not care at all what I thought of them; however, they *did* care what their peers thought.
  - Helping students learn to work collaboratively and cooperatively with peers is the most important skill you can teach in your classroom; it's among the top five skills employers say they want. While it's not easy to teach, it really is worth it. In Chapter 10, "Fair Team Grading Strategies that Work for Humans, we will learn more about how to structure your "compensation" package to motivate students and avoid the dreaded group work pitfalls.
  - It's far from a shirking of your duty as a teacher to have students work in groups or teams. With the proper structure, a team can create conditions necessary for much more powerful learning to occur than any one person could ever accomplish on their own,

but you will have to put measures in place to prevent complacency and promote workload balance. In fact, according to Dr. Kelly-Ann Allen, "Adolescents, in particular, rely on others for approval, decision-making, problem-solving, and social support. Relationships become an important part of identity development and support the transition into young adulthood."[2] This is probably why peer collaboration is so powerful and important for students, especially as they grow into adolescence.

Reflection Activity

What scares you? Specifically, what keeps you from taking the leap and implementing some of the methods we discussed in this chapter. For each method previously used, what is the worst-case scenario if nothing goes right? Now, flip that on its head. What would happen if you were wildly successful with each method we discussed? If you knew you couldn't fail, how much change would it bring to your classroom? I think that most of us will find that the worst-case scenario isn't too bad, especially since we could always go back to how things were if we had no other option. But I hope that we can also agree that the potential for greatness is worth taking that risk.

Strategies and Tools for Improvement

Not everything has to be about technology, but when technology can provide important elements for learning, for example, in the form of motivation factors that are cheap or free, we should use it to its greatest advantage. In some of the preceding examples, I suggested posting to social media or putting videos on YouTube. Depending on the age of your students and the community where you teach, you will need to decide what is acceptable and appropriate. The standards and expectations vary wildly. There are teachers with social media accounts actively used on a daily basis to show student work to parents; there are others who show student work to the world, and both methods can be motivational and safe. I want to address a concern I hear in elementary schools from time to time when I suggest using social media to connect with community members or parents. Sometimes, I'm met with what can best be described as horror. The general takeaway is that displaying photos of students on social media is akin to inviting kidnappers or school shooters into classrooms, and frankly, that is ridiculous. I've asked the most adamant critics to show me any newspaper article or other legitimate news of a single instance of kidnapping or a single school shooting where an adult used social media to applaud student work or citizenship was in any way an inciting element. No one has ever been able to produce such evidence, and after doing my own research, I don't believe there is any.

Today's students live, and have always lived, in a world filled with user-created content; I'm not concluding a judgment on this, it's simply a fact of life for them. Every modern school district has a photo release form on file for every student, and most of them have an opt-out-only mechanism so that, by default, all students are opted in to being photographed and featured on district media outlets. If this is the norm, why not take advantage of the opportunity to draw the outside world in? Why not post student projects to your classroom Instagram account and see which gets the most likes, no names given! Can your grandma spot yours without your help?! Might this not be an interesting experiment? Might it be inspiring for many students who dream of being social media stars like their YouTube or TikTok heroes? I think it might, and contrary to what some will say, it is not a dangerous or immoral practice to post student work online, and fear-based statements that it is cannot withstand scrutiny. On the other hand, there are many good reasons to allow the context of the "real world" into our learning environments. We staunchly insist that schools exist in order to "prepare students for the REAL WORLD," which is a stunning admission that there is nothing much "real" about the school world. We should, if real-world preparation is the goal, be bringing in as many elements of it as are age-appropriate, possible, and useful for our students' growth, development, and motivation.

I want to refer to a part of the lyrics of a song by education technology leader Kevin Honeycutt. It's called "I Need My Teachers to Learn 2.1," and you can find it on You-Tube at https://fried.tech/need-2-learn. I hope you give it a listen.

> In detention hall, there's a quiet young man, head hung low with a phone in hand. It's time to tell his parents 'bout the school's outrage 'cause he tried to post the essay on his Facebook page. He was hoping more people could have read those words 'cause an audience of one, well, it's so absurd. Whatever happened to compromise? He said, "The school should realize."

> These kids are changin', any fool can tell, and the way that you're teachin' has to change as well. You might not like it 'cause we grow up fast, but prepare us for the future and not your past. There's not one minute to burn. We need our teachers to learn.

Takeaways

1. The word *worksheet* represents a mindset about education that often holds us back from maximizing success in our classrooms. Getting beyond the worksheet mindset can improve the student experience, the teacher experience, and the school system as a whole.

2. The difference between delegation and empowerment feels subtle only when you're doing it unto others; when it is done unto you, you will quickly notice it. Design assignments with empathy for those who will complete them and notice this subtle but powerful difference. If the assignment is designed for the trash can, your students will likely treat it as such.

3. The "real world" is not a fictional location that only serves as a hollow reminder of the much more real "school world" we're currently living in. Use everything you can about the real world to improve the school world and don't be deterred by fearmongers if you have an instinct that will help your students get motivated.

Notes

1. DeHartchuck, L. (2021) Positive behavior strategies: An approach for engaging and motivating students. Reports and Students: National Center for Learning Disabilities.

2. Allen, Kelly-Ann (2022). The power of relationships in schools. *Psychology Today*. Chirashree, G. (2012). Role of ICT in improving the quality of school education in Bihar. ELDIS.

CHAPTER EIGHT

Student Choice Continuum and Why Choice Matters

I typically assume that everyone who has a significant other in their life has had, and won, an argument with them at one point or another. I emerged victoriously (picture a female medieval knight) from an argument that I am never going to let go. In fact, I'm devoting a whole chapter to it. It was a Saturday night and my husband, Rich, now a retired educator but a principal at the time of this argument that I won (I'll probably remind you that I won a few times more in this chapter), was driving down the interstate. Maybe it was the wrong time to start an argument (is there ever a right time?), but if you think that would stop me, you don't know me very well yet.

I had noticed in my work as a teacher of both adults and children (at that time I was a district-level Instructional Technology Coordinator) that, no matter the age of a person, the amount of choice they perceived themselves to have seemed to automatically generate or destroy engagement—the more choices, the more engagement naturally emerged.

Before we continue, let's define what is meant by the controversial and extremely overused word *engagement*. When I use the word *engagement*, I'm using it by the definition of Dr. Phillip C. Schlechty:

Engagement

- The student sees the activity as personally meaningful.
- The student's level of interest is sufficiently high that he persists in the face of difficulty.
- The student finds the task sufficiently challenging that she believes she will accomplish something of worth by doing it.
- The student's emphasis is on optimum performance and on "getting it right."

It's hard to understand engagement, though, if you don't know about strategic compliance, so, again from the work of Dr. Schlechty:

Strategic Compliance

- The official reason for the work is not the reason the student does the work—she substitutes her own goals for the goals of the work.
- The substituted goals are instrumental—grades, class rank, college acceptance, parental approval.
- The focus is on what it takes to get the desired personal outcome rather than on the nature of the task itself—satisfactions are extrinsic.
- If the task doesn't promise to meet the extrinsic goal, the student will abandon it.

Dr. Schlechty has five total descriptors for levels of engagement; here is what he calls each of them in descending order:

- Engagement
- Strategic Compliance
- Ritual Compliance

- Retreatism

- Rebellion

Dr. Schlechty posits that by carefully designing work that incorporates student choice and takes into account contextual factors, teachers can help their students become engaged in the work at hand and this increases their learning ability exponentially.

And finally, through my own experience and experimentation, I've found his work to be both helpful and true. This understanding of engagement and design has underpinned every design process I've done in my life. BUT, let's get back to the story of the argument (that I won).

We were speeding down the freeway, and I made the following statement: "The more choices people have, the more naturally engaged they will be." That's one of the reasons why learning theories like Project-Based Learning and Problem Based-Learning are so powerful. Yes, the problem statement or scenario may be defined for you, but how you achieve it is not. That's a lot of choice! Meanwhile, an assignment like a worksheet has no variance. You can't even tell if students have cheated on them because, by definition, the answers should all be the same. Standardization and lack of choice are what make education miserable. Meanwhile, everything fun has lots of choices and decisions. That's when Rich made this statement: "Yeah! That's why science experiments are so great!" (Cue the tense game show finale music.)

"Um, no, science experiments can be really great. They are hands-on, but if you think about schoolwork on a continuum with the amount of choices being the differentiator, then science experiments do not have the most choice. You might get to pick when you dump a beaker or insert a slide, but next time you hear a science teacher say, 'Hey, everybody, just mix a bunch of chemicals together and let's see what happens!' give me a call because I want to come watch the inevitable explosion. Science experiments are very carefully planned, almost always by the teacher, and while I will grant you that they are way better and more engaging than worksheets, I think it's because they are hands-on and not because students are usually making that many choices." This is how I won the argument (hah!), so now you know, I can be a petty and small person who is holding on to years-old arguments and now memorializing them in a book. (Just kidding, but this discussion really did help both of us define how choice plays a role in engagement, and yet, hands-on activities also naturally engage learners.)

Out of this discussion came an important tool called The Student Choice Continuum (shown in Figure 8.1), and

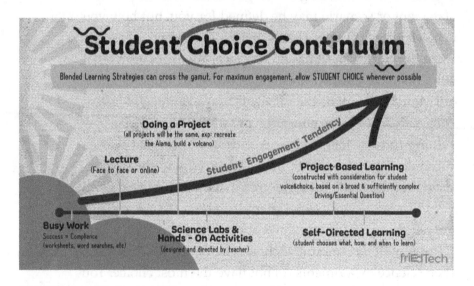

FIGURE 8.1 The Student Choice Continuum tool.

it helped me describe and explain why worksheets, of all school assignments, deserve to die the most.

You see, as a teacher and (also almost certainly) an instructional designer, creating student choice without inviting chaos feels extremely frightening. EVEN IF things in your classroom already aren't going well, you will still be afraid they could get even worse. Until I felt like I hit my own personal version of teaching rock bottom, I wasn't willing to try anything new because even if I was just barely surviving, at least I WAS surviving.

When I polled teachers about what fears they have around giving students more choices, these are the responses that I heard most often:

- They won't know what to do.
- They won't learn anything.
- They won't need me.
- I would get fired.
- My evaluator would give me terrible scores.
- They will just sit there and do nothing.
- My students don't care enough to do this.
- I don't have enough devices.
- I am the expert, so I have to be in charge of what and how people learn.
- What I've always done is working.
- That's not the way we do it (*translation TTWWADI*).
- Parents would complain.

If this type of data interests you, you can also participate in this poll, if you choose to, through the following URL. Or even better, you can copy the poll and use it in your own school to initiate discussions on who is owning the learning in your school: https://fried.tech/bw-who-owns-learning. You'll be able to see the results after you submit your form. Or, you can grab a blank copy of the form at this URL https://fried.tech/bw-owns-learning-copy.

My point is this: it is important for all of us to begin discussing why helping students get engaged in their own learning is so important and how giving students more choices clearly connects with that idea.

I'll tell you though, one of the most exhausting things about giving students who aren't used to choices a bunch of choices is all of the wearying questions you will get as a teacher. From "What color pen do you want me to write with" to "Do you want me to write my name in the top left or the top right," concluding, always, with "Can I go to the bathroom now." Decision fatigue is one of the most difficult things about being a teacher. I can't tell you how many days early in my career I couldn't make one more decision after I left school. Even "what should we make for dinner" might set me off on a tirade because I had made SO MANY CHOICES that, by the end of the day, I was just DONE. In the next chapter, I'm going to tell you more about how I solved this problem with the "Question Slip" I showed you in Chapter 4. For me, it was such a life-changer that I'm bringing it to the surface at least three times in this book, so stay tuned.

Teacher Work

As students, we probably grew up in a world where we thought of our teachers as people who knew things we did not know. The job of "teacher" was to convey those "things" to students; naturally students were the people who did not know. With the advent of the internet (which in early days required a person to be able to read) and now video platforms like YouTube (which do not even require that skill), anyone can be the one who knows (or thinks they know) something. This shift, more than any other, has turned the traditional dynamic of "teacher" and "student" on its side, leaving many of us upended. What is still true, however, is that the person who is making all of the decisions is the person probably doing most of the work and who is, as a consequence, also probably the person doing most of the learning.

To illustrate this point, I'm thinking back to a college class I took that was advertised to be about classroom technology; it was around 1993 though, and classroom "technology" was not very advanced. My awful professor, Dr. Schwartz, was behind the times even by 1990s standards. In one unit, for example, we learned to use one of those blackline master machines, which should tell you how behind he really was. I'm guessing many of you don't even know what I'm talking about. At the time, I was substitute teaching in the town where I was attending university and had been on several school campuses. I had never seen such a machine in any of the workrooms, so it was clearly already outdated. In this course, Dr. Schwartz essentially had us make, and duplicate, our own worksheets. True confession, it was SO FUN making worksheets, and since my understanding of how paltry these intended assignments were was years and years away, I got to fully enjoy the experience of creating them. I did all of my assignments on the subject of learning the French language, which I literally have a degree in but can barely speak (throat clear) though I completed all the worksheets. I used this subject for two reasons: first, it was more fun to create worksheets about vocabulary; learning discrete topics like this lent itself to the worksheet very well, and second, Dr. Schwartz didn't know anything about it (BONUS). The point is, I have three college credit hours in, basically, creating worksheets and copying them using ancient technology, so, as you can see, I am well-qualified in this area. Tee hee!

I wonder if this series of activities has you thinking about TPT, Teachers Pay Teachers. On this website, teachers, beleaguered, exhausted, and sometimes poor as they are, create, upload, buy, and sell worksheets. (If you're an educator, this is NOT the first you've heard of it, and if you're NOT an educator and you're reading this book, we're probably related. Hi family!) I'm not saying that everything for sale on TPT is a worksheet, but I am saying that TPT is famous, or infamous, as a worksheet factory. If I still believed in worksheets, I could make some and upload them for SURE because I truly enjoy that process. In Dr. Schwartz's class, I drew little pictures, picked out fonts, and now you can even use colors because they're mostly meant to be digital. Oh, man, what fun! BUT, spoiler, I would be the only one learning. I didn't figure that out until I actually taught French and thought I would try to use the awful stuff I made in Dr. Schwartz's crappy class, you know, to save time. I learned so much making those things, but my students just had a few minutes of busy work to do; it was abundantly clear that learning was not happening for them like it had for me during the creation process. (I still give zero stars to Dr. Schwartz for his teaching. I learned about

French vocabulary, not anything related to "technology.")
I had to ask myself why. Why, if I had learned so much in
creating the worksheets, were they learning just as little by
actually completing them? Well, the answer led to another
profound realization about worksheets: the only person
who is going to learn anything and actually have to do any
critical thinking is the person making the worksheets.

The Upside-Down Worksheet

This led me to try a new type of assignment where students
would create worksheets and then trade and complete them
for each other, then after completion, finally discuss how
that process had gone and reflect on what they'd learned. It
was a lot more fun and a ton more learning took place! Yes,
it took light years longer than the busy work I had given
them, BUT, light years more learning happened too, so that
was okay. My original worksheet creation from college was
about family vocabulary. I had drawn a family and labeled
everyone with their appropriate vocabulary word in English
and left a space for students to write the corresponding article (le, la—every noun in French has a gender) and word in
French, *father* = *le père*, *sister* = *la soeur*, and so on. The activity of drawing, then labeling, then thinking about what the
answers were was both fun and educational, so why not
have my students do it and benefit from that process? I did,
and it was actually pretty cool and probably one of the first
times in my career I appropriately "killed" a worksheet.

If TPT had existed at that time, I could have downloaded
something from it; thank goodness it did not exist because

it might have delayed my acceptance that that kind of assignment didn't work well at all, especially if I had spent hard-earned money there. True, the TPT version would likely have been nicely formatted and easy for the students to read and comprehend, but having students do the work themselves, looking up the words and making the answer keys, was profoundly better as a learning experience. The performance aspect of having the kids trade papers and do each other's worksheets turned out to be pretty cool too. "What did you expect me to put here if that isn't right?" they'd ask and the reply might be something like, "Well, you can't tell if this baby is a brother or a sister or what, so I thought you would come up with *le bébé* (*baby*) or *l'enfant* (*child*) instead of *le frère* (*brother*), I mean, I guess it's not wrong, but it's not what I thought you would put." What a great discussion where both parties are really thinking about the vocabulary and looking at things from another person's perspective.

Let's take this newly revised assignment back to the Student Choice Continuum. Where do you think it might fall? In the example I gave you, I defined the vocabulary as "family," so I took that choice away from the students, but there are still a lot of choices left. If I showed students an example of the worksheet I made in college, they would see I'd drawn a picture. That would imply to them that their work also needed to have a picture but unless I told them this, it would still be their choice to make. I could circumvent this by using some more complex topic without really clear connections between the words and not showing an example, but I might wait to do that until I've tried this method with a class a few times first. They could choose which vocabulary words from the list they addressed; maybe I would give them 20 but they would only need to address 10. They could choose how they wanted to construct their worksheet. If they were using technology, they could choose fonts and colors, and pictures from the internet, icons, or emojis to represent their vocabulary. I probably would not let most groups choose who would be the partner(s) to do the worksheets because there would be too many ways for someone to get left out, but there are still a lot of choices to be made. By the time my students hit their sophomore or junior years of high school, they had tons of experience with worksheets. Strangely, when you first implement an upside-down assignment like this in your classroom, you may have students who react with something called learned helplessness, but before we move on to that important topic, let's take a moment to reflect.

Journaling Activity

Think of some projects, assignments, or activities that you have completed with students in the past. Referring back to the Student Choice Continuum chart, where do each of these activities fall? I encourage you to create a copy of this chart: https://fried.tech/bw-student-choice. On the second slide, you will find a blank version. Add some different activities or assignments onto the chart itself. Thinking about each of those activities, do you find that your students were typically more engaged the further to the right the activity fell on the chart? Why do you think this is, beyond what we have already discussed?

Learned Helplessness and the Worksheet

Learned helplessness is "a condition in which a person has a sense of powerlessness, arising from a traumatic event or persistent failure to succeed" (*Oxford English Dictionary*). For students who have not been asked to learn without worksheets before, an assignment like the "Upside-Down Worksheet" with all its choices can be utterly overwhelming, but as teachers, we have to help our students through this overwhelmed state. When I first stopped using worksheets, my students swiftly rebelled. I had to call the counselor and ask her to give me a couple of weeks before honoring schedule change request forms! They were really upset that I was asking them to "do so much work" while I "did nothing!" Another thing I heard was, "Miss, this is YOUR job. YOU are supposed to make the worksheets; we're just supposed to DO them. Just give us a packet!" Not all students responded this way, but there were always some. At the time, I sort of wondered if I was going to get in trouble with parents, or even worse, be that teacher no one liked. What I know now, though, and what I've hopefully reflected well to you, is that the person who is doing the most work is doing the most learning, and I never, ever had a student who didn't eventually come around to my way of thinking on that. When people finally experience the success of learning, they can't help but be proud of themselves, and those who have been the most traumatized by previous unsuccessful schooling are the most convinced, once they see that when provided the right experiences and context for the work of learning, they really can learn quite well.

It's worth remembering, too, that if you're worried the wheels will fly off the proverbial bus if you give students too many choices, then just start smaller. Start having students make choices for themselves in small ways first; not all choices need to be big ones. "Can I write with this pen or do I need to use a pencil?" type questions, once eliminated from your day, will leave you extra brain space and energy you weren't even aware you were missing, and why does it really matter what writing utensil a student uses, in most cases? A teacher I once knew (George Pitlik, I see you!) got himself a laser pointer and put up three signs in his room, YES, NO, YOU DECIDE. When a student asked him a question like this, one of those that doesn't really necessarily warrant an answer that matters, he would just point the laser pointer at the answer. Most of the time it was YOU DECIDE, and that was that. Soon, those types of questions faded and students started asking him better questions. If you're thinking maybe you're too big a control freak to live with that type of chaos, but you're also feeling overwhelmed by the sheer number of decisions you feel like you have to make on a daily basis, consider whether it's really worth it to be controlling the type and number of things you are in your classroom. Practice letting some small things go and teaching your students to decide those things for themselves.

Reflection Activity

Knowing what you know now, how might you change some of those activities you previously thought of that fell more to the left of the Student Choice Continuum? Remember, if you feel like you are doing the majority of the work, there is probably a better way to get the students to be more involved in the learning process. It might be more difficult to achieve, but it will be worth it when you see students who previously were disengaged truly get excited about creating and learning content. Push yourself to give your students as many decisions as possible, and then relax a little while you watch them flourish.

Takeaways

1. Choices are important for humans to get invested in what they are doing and one of the reasons worksheets don't "work" is because they take away too many choices from the learner, decreasing engagement to levels not measurable with the current available equipment.

2. Using Schlechty's definition of *engagement* when thinking about or discussing educational matters helps us add precision to our dialogue so that *engaged* is not interchangeable with simply *entertained*.

3. The number of decisions (choices) teachers make on a daily basis is staggering. There's an unscientific infographic you can find at https://fried.tech/teacher-choices that illustrates teachers make an average of 1,500 decisions per day.[1] When we know that many of those choices don't matter to the learning process but they could increase engagement if left to students

instead, this is good data to use to make a change that benefits both us and our students' learning.

Note

1. Contributor, B. (Ed.). (2016, February 15). Teachers—the real masters of multitasking: Infographic. *Busy Teacher*. https://busyteacher. org/16670-teachers-masters-of-multitasking-infographic.html

Stop Stealing the Learning

If I can't reiterate ONE more term today to make you groan, my name isn't Amy Mayer. Let's do this! *Student-centered learning*: if you had no professional development or bad professional development, it means that you, the educator, don't matter AT ALL in the equation of the school environment, you are NOT a variable. Give up ALL your nights, weekends, and bathroom breaks. Create a different lesson plan for every student. Nod vigorously and use the words *student-centered* a lot in conversation. Ask questions in staff meetings, "Is that really 'student-centered' though?" (Raise your eyebrows and slightly cock your head when you say this for maximum effect.) These are all ways to fake student-centered learning since what you were taught (or not taught) is completely impossible to execute. This kind of double life you've been living has GOT to end.

Honestly, one of the most stressful parts of teaching is having to live the lie of understanding and implementing the district's latest buzzwords, which will inevitably change the following year, continuing the never-ending cycle. For me personally, it was a close kinsman of student-centered learning, possibly its mother? I'm sure some of you will recognize her, she was called "differentiated instruction." I went to workshops for a couple of years about differentiated instruction and I never did find out what it was while I was a classroom teacher. It was probably another couple of years after working in curriculum and instruction, and other adjacent positions, that I finally understood what it meant (and that it wasn't meant to kill the teacher). I've got it now, and I'm ready to explain it to you in terms that will make you an honest person again.

What Is *Student-Centered* Supposed to Mean?

Student-centered learning is, in reality, the only kind of learning there is. Education used to be thought of similarly to computer programming: I tell this content (lesson = x), they do this (worksheet = y), they regurgitate it (test = z), and this is learning; problem solved ($x + y = z$). However, we now know that for today's students, this formula simply isn't working, and frankly, I don't think that it is working very well for educators either. Students are not computers; they are complicated individuals who bring an entire life, no matter how short, of experiences into our classrooms. Instead of dreaming and wishing this wasn't the case, we can leverage those experiences to actually help our students to learn more effectively. In fact, we have *no choice* but to figure this out or leave the profession, and I don't say that lightly. As you all now know, I faced that choice myself and the ONLY reason I'm still an educator today is because there was a crappy job market at the time, and I couldn't find something else to pay the bills. BUT, I'm so thankful that there wasn't because, through this, I figured out how to do this thing that I now know is called student-centered instruction.

You got an introduction to how I began considering student-centered instruction in my own classroom already. Over the years, my understanding of what it was and how to do it has expanded exponentially. Right now, my guess is that you are doing a *LOT* more work than your students, and you can feel that imbalance. You feel like a mule driver behind a team of mules who spends your days screaming at the poor beasts with all your might, but they aren't moving, or worse, they're running in 10 different directions. It's the hardest job in the world and you have to do it period after period, day after day. It's time to STOP. THE. MADNESS. And get THEM following YOU instead of the other way around.

So, how do you do it? Like we did when we started on the worksheet-killing journey together: we have to change the question we're asking. Let's keep it really simple to start; instead of following the left-hand column in the following table, follow the right-hand model. . . .

Worksheet Thinking	Worksheet-Killer Thinking
I will create a presentation to teach the causes of the Civil War.	Students will research and debate the causes of the Civil War.
I will create a worksheet to practice fractions.	Students will create problems their classmates will solve.
I will create a Kahoot to introduce the novel.	Students will create Kahoots about their favorite background topics for the novels they choose.

Worksheet Thinking	Worksheet-Killer Thinking
I will find a video to introduce volcanos.	Students will search for and identify the best video and most reliable, interesting, and factual website to introduce volcanos.
I will find an example of a model paragraph and explain why.	Students will find and explain why their choice is a good example of a "perfect" paragraph.

If you are thinking, "Well, if they knew how to do *THAT* then they wouldn't need *ME*" then you may be surprised to hear that you are on the right track. The thing is, if you have internet access in your classroom and at least a few devices (notice they do not have to be a certain kind of device, even some smartphones will do), then you can start to put the students in charge of their own learning and make yourself the guide on the side.

Journaling Activity

I want you to take a moment and think back to the Student Choice Continuum that we discussed in the previous chapter and how it related to student-centered learning. As we previously discussed, worksheets very clearly fall to the far left of this continuum, where students have no choice, and by relation, limited to no learning is achieved, and engagement is not naturally created. Specifically, think about how giving up some control (i.e., not doing all of the work) can lead to wild success in student learning by creating a truly student-centered learning environment.

In this journal entry, I ask you to answer the following questions:

- Why are we afraid to give up control in our classrooms? Is it because of our own fears, or how we fear we will be viewed by the students, parents, or administration?

- What is the worst-case scenario for each group we fear will judge us and find us lacking?

- How can you challenge those fears in the work you do daily in the classroom? For example, can you say, with authority, to a parent that you are doing what you are absolutely positive is best for their student's future? If so, that is a strong statement to use to confront a fear you may have.

- What wild successes might you have if you fully let go of this fear?

Take a Trip to Centered

In order to understand how this change may look as you continue your journey to transform your classroom from a teacher-centered to a more centered environment, let's look at a bold scenario. You may not want to dive in to the degree Mrs. Ferrer does, but I hope this story will give you some ideas just the same.

Mrs. Ferrer is once again struggling to start class in her 5th-grade science classroom, just like every other day. Even though the bell already rang, her students are still trickling in and engaged in conversations about the weekend, boys, girls, and so on. "Here we go again," she thinks with a slight hope soon things will be changing. It's time to get started on understanding scientific practices, one of the most important, and difficult, things she will teach this year. This standard includes designing experiments that isolate a variable and reporting direct and inferred evidence, among other things. (She chuckles a little inwardly at the thought of these kids actually being able to do that learning on their own, or at all. If she doesn't laugh, she might cry.) Well, it's time to take the first step in shifting from being the "mule driver" to the "mule whisperer."

"Hi, everyone, please take your seats. I have a big announcement, and it's important that you all hear it and get your questions answered in the next 30 minutes because something big is happening." Huh, how about that, sensing a change, they do start to settle rather quickly. Mrs. Ferrer passes out team assignments while she explains that everyone must change seats and sit with their new team members. Labels are already on the desks. There's a lot of grumbling and it's getting louder, so she reminds everyone that the big announcement is coming as soon as everyone is seated, but they don't have much time. Several minutes go by with grumbling and scraping of stools, but soon it grows uncharacteristically quiet.

Mrs. Ferrer begins, "I don't know about you, but for me, this class hasn't been very much fun. It's not something I look forward to each day. I don't feel like you've been learning very much and that bothers me a lot." Students start to try to catch the eyes of their friends across the room. Did they drive another teacher out of teaching already this year? Mrs. Ferrer continues, "From now on, I want you to consider this classroom your place of employment. Now, I can't pay you, but. . ." a few kids chuckle. . ."but," Mrs. Ferrer continues, "I can do better at giving you a learning experience where you'll be motivated to succeed. From now on, you are going to do more work than me." (Groans emanate from several places around the classroom.) "From now on, YOU will be in charge of teaching each other what we have to learn in this class. I will help you by giving you timelines and topics that you will need, but you, every single one of you, will be responsible for putting together what your classmates will learn and constructing how they will learn it. In a few minutes I'll give you a chance to ask all the questions you want, but right now, I have to tell you about another tool we'll be implementing as of today."

Mrs. Ferrer was already reflecting in a part of her brain that this class had never been this quiet for this long, and that was a very good thing.

As she starts to pass out small slips of paper, Mrs. Ferrer continues, "Okay, these little slips of paper I'm giving you, three per group of four students, four for the group of five students, is called a 'Question Slip.' Like I told you, my role in this classroom is changing. I'm going to be here to help you, but mostly to listen and guide you so that what you're teaching your classmates is as clear and correct as it can be. I realize sometimes you're going to have questions you can't just Google or that you'll need resources you need my help to find. When that happens, you will use these Question Slips" (Figure 9.1).

"A Question Slip is a way to ask a question outside of Free Question Time, which we are about to practice in a few minutes and will do every day. In order to use the Question Slip, all members of a four-person team who are present or four members of a five-person team must sign the slip and hand it to me at the time the question is asked. Just because you

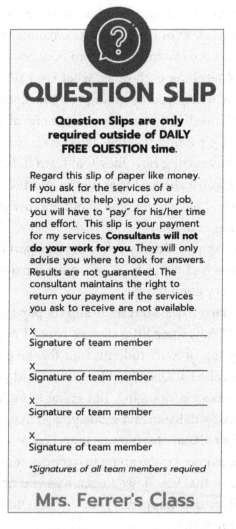

FIGURE 9.1 A template for this file can be found in the ancillary materials at https://fried.tech/bw-question.

fill out a Question Slip doesn't mean I'll be able to answer your question, but I promise that I will do my best to help you. I want to emphasize again, once I give your teams your assignments, they are *YOUR* assignments. I'm not going to do them for you like I have been all school year."

Mrs. Ferrer sees a few satisfying nods of heads. Everyone is making direct eye contact with her. This feels pretty good, and a little scary. She knows the real pushback is coming, but gets a sensation it is going to be well worth it.

Mrs. Ferrer has prepared project briefs for her students. Each team receives a different project brief and a place on that brief where they can add a team name and the team members' names. Each one also comes in a standard manila folder, gotta love old-school style! "Before you leave each day, it's my advice you put your team folder into this box, but that's up to you. If you choose not to do that, and whoever takes it home doesn't bring it back, the whole team will be forced to start over. This project is going to take about two weeks. If you can't get it done during class time, you will have to work on it on your own time." Mrs. Ferrer indicates the box. Although she wants to say this several more times, she stops herself. After all, the whole idea of this new experiment is to have the students be responsible for their own learning.

Mrs. Ferrer then gives a general overview of different parts of the project brief, explains the job titles of each team member, the goals of the team as well as the due dates, benchmarks, and individual grades. Once she feels this is enough new information for one day, she realizes that there have still been no interruptions, and she still can't believe this class (*THIS CLASS!*) has been quiet and attentive for this long. She decides it's time to give them time to ask questions and then begin to digest the information within their teams. "All right, that's probably enough new information for one day. Today, your team needs to read the job descriptions and make sure everyone understands their roles and work together to decide a team name. (Mrs. Ferrer indicates the board with this directive written on it with her hand.)

Tomorrow we'll actually begin the work. Now, and for as long as it takes, it's Free Question Time. Once Free Question Time is over, your team will need to provide a Question Slip to get a question answered. Everybody got it?" She sees lots of nodding. Joseph is the first to speak up,

"Miss, if we are going to be doing all the work from now on, then why are they paying you?" As he intended, there are several snickers from a couple of areas of the room and a hearty "Yeah!" But Mrs. Ferrer was prepared for this.

"Guys, it's my job to get you to learn. What I have been doing was sure teaching me a lot, but you guys have hardly learned anything. I found out I was actually stealing your learning from you by doing all that work. I feel bad about it, but there's nothing I can do now except make a change. Now I know that the person who does all the learning is the one who does the work, and I'm going to make sure that's you from now on."

Emma's hand had been up the entire time Mrs. Ferrer was speaking, stretching high and waving ever so slightly with tension, so she doubted Emma had heard anything she'd said. "Emma?" Mrs. Ferrer said.

"I always end up doing all the work anytime I'm in a group and it's not fair!" Well, maybe it wasn't the very best way for Emma to share this information, but Mrs. Ferrer knew this would come up eventually, and once again, she was prepared.

"Look, everyone, it's my job to make sure you learn the concepts of this subject and grade level AND that you learn to think and learn independently so that when I'm not there, you still know how to do what we studied in this class. I have a way to make sure that you get a grade that reflects *your* efforts. Now, as I told you, we're not going to go over that today because we have already discussed so many new things, so you'll have to trust me on this, we will soon. Emma, I hope I've earned enough trust from you that you can wait a few days to understand how that's going to work, okay?"

"Now, what else is there?" Again, this was the most quiet this class had ever been and they were 30 minutes into the 50-minute period. "Okay, I'll leave Free Question Time open for one minute or as long as questions keep coming in, then I'll ask for a Question Slip after that time. Anyone else have a question?" No hands went up; no one spoke. "Okay, let's get to work, teams," Mrs. Ferrer ended. How long would it take before she had one of those Question Slips back? Five minutes? Surely before the class period ended. Mrs. Ferrer headed back to her desk to make sure she had completed the attendance report for today. Did she forget with her own anticipation? Probably.

No more than three minutes later, Mia was at her desk. "Miss, can I go to the bathroom?"

"Mia, that's a question, may I have the slip?"

"Uh, no ma'am. Never mind."

This might be working too well, Mrs. Ferrer thought to herself. "Okay, Mia, if you REALLY have to go, you should let me know; otherwise, we line up in less than 10 minutes and you can go then, okay?"

Mia nodded and returned to her seat. Mrs. Ferrer could see the other students immediately asking her how it went, and Mia explaining that the Question Slip was indeed requested. Huh, this was getting sincerely interesting. Mrs. Ferrer began walking around the perimeter of the room listening to the conversations happening about team names and asking each other questions about the job descriptions. José turned around in his seat as Mrs. Ferrer passed by.

"Hey, miss, what does *Notetaker* mean, like, besides that I have to take notes. Is that all I have to do to get a grade?" Mrs. Ferrer reached out her arm with her hand out, palm up.

"Question Slip?" she enquired. José's shoulders slumped as he turned back to his team.

"Hey, y'all, I need to ask Mrs. F a question. Sign this." He handed one of the Question Slips to the classmate across from him in the table group who immediately jerked his hands away as if touching a hot stove.

"Dude! I'm not signing anything! She said we're doing this for two weeks. You can ask tomorrow during Open Question time!" The rest of the group nodded along in agreement.

There were three minutes left till the bell. Mrs. Ferrer glanced around the room and saw Mia, who appeared to be happily writing the team name for her group on the team dossier. As the Notetaker, that was indeed part of her job. "Okay, everyone, please make sure to put your team name on the tab of your folder so you can slip it into the box on the way out. It's almost time to line up." She heard a couple of groans and a small voice say, "Oh, my gosh, we have so much to do. Do we HAVE to go to PE?" Wow, Mrs. Ferrer had never heard anything like that before. Maybe this wild idea was going to work after all!

On the way back from dropping her class off in the gym for PE, Mrs. Ferrer reflected that there would likely be some hard days ahead with this new way of teaching, but that the first step seemed to go remarkably well, certainly much better than she had expected.

Becoming a Worksheet Killer

Mrs. Ferrer would be right in thinking that the hard parts had not yet arrived. Especially with students who have been raised on worksheets and spoon-fed every bite of knowledge since kindergarten, there can be quite a bit of resentment when moving to a truly student-centered learning environment where the students are doing the majority of the work of learning. I also want to say that when you say "student-centered teaching" to people who are not Worksheet Killers, they are likely not going to think you mean what you actually mean, and that's okay. If you decide to jump off this diving board and give it a try, these are the things I would like you to keep in mind:

- The person doing the work is the only one doing the learning. If you are a teacher, the person doing the work must be the students.

- Evaluation is not the same as learning; just because you are not evaluating it does not mean learning isn't happening. Extremely valuable learning often happens during team discussions, for example; these are not likely to be evaluated.

- You don't have to be in control of everything; in fact, if you are, you will not have a student-centered learning environment. Just because the learning is not happening with the trajectory you planned doesn't mean it isn't happening.

- If teams are going on a tangent you didn't intend and it's not part of the learning you outlined, it's perfectly fine to redirect, but the conversations should be more question-based than dictatorial. For example, the team in charge of teaching "Reasonable Explanations" is instead discussing the existence, or lack thereof, of UFOs. Mrs. Ferrer is well within her role to redirect by asking, "Do you guys think this one example is going to do enough to teach everyone about reasonable explanations or should it be just one example of what you're talking about?"

- The younger students are and the less experienced they are at learning on their own, the more help they will need with smaller deadlines closer together and with peer-to-peer interactions. Soft skills lessons will be necessary as will small, attainable deadlines that, if missed, will not derail the entire project. One idea is to keep the rest of your instruction the same while trying a mini-project in one subject to start out. Then, teamwork time will be limited to that subject's time.

- Students with learning disabilities will still need extra support; hopefully, this model will give you more time to work with them in small group settings.

- If you work in a school with high parent involvement, you should inform parents in advance about the Question Slip. Make sure everyone is aware of "Free Question Time" and that it occurs every day. Make sure stakeholders know that as soon as Question Slips are used, more will be forthcoming, on a daily basis if needed. Explain that you are not actually trying to decrease questions, but instead, to improve the quality of questions. Instead of "Can I use a blue pen instead of a pencil," you will be answering questions about the content and learning. It's important to reassure parents that you are helping their students become more independent learners and thinkers and that you truly have their child's best interest at heart.

Finally, I'll ask you to remember that this method is not going to "work" overnight. Just like anything else, it requires you to stick to your principles about the basic tenet (*the person doing the work is doing the learning*), don't "take over" when it's not immediately working or you will be *stealing the learning*. The other "things" you have to teach, seemingly as a result of this change, that is, teamwork, compromise, appropriate communication, meeting deadlines, and so on, are extremely important lessons, as important as your content, and you would have to teach them anyway in any sort of student-centered learning environment. Be strong, this is what it takes to finally kill the worksheet.

Reflection Activity

Reflecting about the scenario that we just went over in Mrs. Ferrer's classroom, think about the following questions:

- Have you ever had a strong reaction like Mrs. Ferrer's class on starting an activity or project that you facilitated in your classroom?

- If so, what similarities did that project have to the one we explored here? If not, why do you think that might be?

- What could you try tomorrow to dip your toe into this pool of student-centered learning if you aren't ready to cannonball your way in just yet? For example, could you use Question Slips with pairs of learners working together for a short period of time?

Strategies and Tools for Improvement

During my time as a classroom teacher, it became possible, and then later mandatory, for each teacher to have a "website." I say "website" in quotations because usually, what they actually meant was a single landing page with some standard (and not very helpful) information displayed, like conference times and contact information. But for me, this was a wonderful opportunity to have a sustained place for information that students or parents could use to empower themselves without my assistance, and I'm sure it won't surprise you that I am really into that idea. However, in most schools, even where teachers are still required to "have a website" (strangely, this practice has come and then gone already in most schools), the content is not useful to anyone. It's stale and standardized if it exists at all. There is no reason to go to the page other than to perhaps see an old headshot or possibly, though not likely, get an email address. This is so sad to me because a REAL teacher website can be incredibly valuable. If I were teaching today and my school didn't give me an easy way to create one, I would use a tool on my own to do it. I would put the briefs for projects on that site, I would have a calendar, and I would link to reliable websites and other resources for both students and their parents to use to get their questions answered without emailing or calling me. Toward the end of my career in the classroom, I was doing many speaking engagements that took me away from school. I found my class website to be an amazing resource for making sure students knew what to do, when, and how, whether I was in the building or not. After a few months of school had passed and all students knew how to get to the site, when I had a substitute, I was able to tell them that the students could access everything they needed on the website and to leave the URL for them as well. The point is, having a sustained location where all information lives is a major key to achieving balance as a teacher. Here are some example student questions you might be answering 10 to 100 times a day. What if those questions could always be answered, "It's on the website!"

Q: I was absent yesterday, can you tell me what I missed?

A: It's on the website.

Q: I can't find my project brief. Can I get another one?

A: It's on the website.

Q: Miss, what is that website you told us about where we could find the. . . .

A: It's on the website.

I think you see where I'm going with this. The answer was always (ALWAYS) "It's on the website." If I got a question and it wasn't "on the website," the answer was, "Give me a few minutes and it will be on the website." One key to keeping your website up to date is linking to other sources that are dynamic, for example, a calendar you publish through Google Calendars—helpful hint, create a calendar layer for each subject you teach. You can also publish an entire folder of content using either Google or Microsoft. Once you have a folder with resources, set the permissions of the folder to "anyone with the link can view," then grab the URL of the top level folder. On your website, add some helpful text to describe what will be found at the link, like "Click here for current project materials," then link that text to the folder's URL. Now, when you add "stuff" to the folder (or add events to your class calendar), your website will automagically be updated.

Some of you may be thinking, "I have that, and it's an LMS," and if so, you are partially correct! I like having a truly public and accessible place for anyone to use to find information there is no reason to keep private. As a parent myself, my younger child's school used a learning management system to house all of the information, but it was so complicated, and frankly, convoluted that I never logged into it after the first time. If I had been able to access teacher websites, I definitely would have been more informed.

If your district website tool is not allowing you to really use the space, it's too technically difficult, or there is not a district provided website or page, you could consider one or more of the following tools:

Tool Name	Purpose and URL	Things to Consider and Check
Google Sites	Using Google Sites templates, you can create a full-fledged website very quickly with very little technical knowledge. Get started at http://sites.google.com.	Depending on your school district's settings, you may or may not be able to create a Google Site within your district account. Before you invest time in this tool, make sure you can actually make your site public so that it can be used with your target audience. If students have to log in to see your site, that is a major barrier to access. It may also be possible to create the site in your personal Gmail account and give greater access. Combine this site with what you learned earlier about URL shorteners like bit.ly, and you can get a site name like bit.ly/mrs-mayers-class (not a real URL) or similar that your students can remember or easily type in.

Tool Name	Purpose and URL	Things to Consider and Check
Wix.com	Like Google Sites, Wix has a whole world of templates and a free version you can use to create a website easily. While Wix is geared toward business, the tools are robust and the templates are varied enough that you can most likely find one that will work as a starting place at https://fried.tech/bw-wix-edu.	Make sure the Wix website and any websites you create are visible through your school's network, especially if you have noticed many sites are blocked at school. Once again, you can overcome the unwieldy yet free default Wix URL with a URL shortener where you can create a custom URL your students will easily be able to type in.
Wakelet	While Wakelet is not strictly a website builder like the preceding tools, it is easy to learn from a technical perspective and will allow you the ability to have a space online where you can share information and resources with your students. Get started at https://learn.wakelet.com/.	Wakelet is commonly used inside the education space and is probably not blocked on your school's network. At the time of publication, Wakelet has a robust free version that will allow an individual teacher to publish several "collections" for free.

Takeaways

1. Worksheet-Killer Thinking means that we think first about what the students will do in order to learn, and second about our work as teachers.

2. Implementing Question Slips can decrease the number of irrelevant questions you address daily and improve the quality of questions you receive as well as inspiring autonomy among your students.

3. Creating an easily accessible space where nonconfidential information can consistently be found can save untold hours of answering questions and be empowering for students, parents, and even substitute teachers.

CHAPTER TEN

Fair Team Grading Strategies that Work for Humans

What is fair? If you worked at a hypothetical company where everyone got paid the same amount no matter what kind or quality of work they did, my guess is that no matter how high the salary, you would not be happy with that job. If you are an educator, this very well may be the situation you work in, so you're in a good position to determine if it's motivational or not. When I was a teacher, salaries were decided based on years of service, not quality of work or output, which continues to be the case for the vast majority of teaching positions. System designs like this lead to dissatisfaction of employees, a decrease in productivity, and potentially most important, a decrease in our motivation to collaborate.

As a person who has been a student and has likely participated in a "group project" more than once, you will understand why there are so many jokes about the practice. The internet is overflowing with memes created by bitter former students who did "all the work" while their classmates got the grades. One of my favorites is a meme that shows a class picture; underneath it there is a tagline stating, "When I die, I want all the people I worked on group projects with to lower me into the grave so they can let me down one last time." It's funny because it's true, but in order to leverage the tremendous power of teams and collaborative learning, we have to overcome the pitfalls of teamwork, in the workplace, in schools, and in life.

Why We Hate Group Work

Let's start by examining why we all feel some kind of way about "group work." Here are the top five reasons we hate it:

5. Everyone gets the same grade no matter what they put into it.

4. I'm the only one who cares about my grade, so I have to do it all myself.

3. I have nothing to use to motivate the other students I'm supposed to be working with, so I have to do it all myself.

2. My standards are completely different from the rest of my group, so I have to do all the work to meet my own standards.

1. I always have to work with people who have lesser skills than me, so I end up doing all the work.

The even bigger problem than our person who ends up doing all the work is that the rest of the team is presumably also doing nothing, meaning that they learn nothing, totally defeating the purpose of the schooling itself. The person who "did everything," may think they saved the day or should get an extra + after that *A*, but in reality, they inadvertently did more damage than good for their classmates. If our grading system gives them an *A*, it fails the test and if it gives the rest of the group an *A*, it fails again.

The Elements of a Group Project

In order to solve this problem, we have to separate the three elements of a group project: 1) the learning goals, 2) the product (output), and 3) the teamwork. Each of these elements has to be present in order to have a successful project experience. The learning goals are something that need to be independently and individually verified so that if a member of the group doesn't achieve them, they are not inadvertently left out of the learning process. The product/output/demonstration of learning can receive a score, but this should be different from the individual performance of the learning goals. And finally, the teamwork that occurred is a thing unto itself that can be evaluated and improved separately from the other elements of the project.

I hated group learning so much as a student that I initially didn't want to use the strategy as a teacher; I feared no matter how bad things were, this practice would make them even worse. But as I explained in my lightbulb moment story, I couldn't discern a way to help students care about the work and learning without helping them see themselves as part of a system that they were responsible for. I now know that, as human beings, it's important for us psychologically to see ourselves as part of something larger than ourselves, and beyond that, to understand and play our part within that system. Many of the issues in our society today arise because our communities and places within those communities have become uncertain. This is a problem that we can, and should, help fix within our classroom learning environments as teachers and leaders must focus on improving for the success of our larger school and district communities.

The Letter-Writing Campaign

In one of the hardest classes I ever taught (and when I say *hard*, I mean it was hard because of the mix of students in the group and their personalities), I had to do some community work to help students see each other as fellow human beings. Frankly, I needed some help seeing them as fellow human beings, too. A teacher friend of mine had attended a training session covering the Capturing Kids' Hearts program. No matter what you think about that program, and it's not without controversy now, there are some good ideas presented there. One she brought back to me was called the letter-writing campaign. Disclaimer: I have no idea if this is how CKH suggests this project should go. I never got to attend the training; I just learned about it during duty one day in the hallway and decided I would try it in my own way. BUT, I did understand that my "community of learners" was not the sort of community anyone would want to be a part of and agreed in my heart that I should do whatever I could to decrease the animosity in the room. I bought a mailbox at Home Depot and created an initial letter to my students. It went something like this:

> Dear Students,
>
> There are so many things that I like and notice about each of you each day. In an effort to get us better connected to each other, we will be writing letters to each other a few times a week. I will assign you someone to write to who will not know they are assigned to you. It will be your job to observe that person, try to get to know them, etc., so that when you write them a letter, you will have something personal and meaningful to say. Letters may only focus on positive observations

and cannot just be focused on generalities. For example, I can't just write:

"Natalie, I think you're nice. —Amy"

but I can write,

"Natalie, I noticed that you always lend your teammates pencils and pens when they don't have them and that's pretty cool of you. Thank you for being a thoughtful and prepared person. —Amy"

The thing is, the first message (you're nice) doesn't mean much. There is no REASON why I think that, so it's a meaningless generality. The second letter is specific. (I think you're nice because I have observed you doing this nice thing.) The first letter doesn't mean much to me, the second one I care about quite a bit more.

What do you do if you get assigned to write a letter to someone you don't particularly like? Well, you find something to like about them in your observations.

Can you write to other people who are not assigned to you? YES, you can write as many letters as you like as long as you also write your required letters.

Can we write to you, Ms. Mayer? YES, while you will not be assigned to write to me, I will be writing letters too and would love to get letters from you.

Sincerely,

Ms. Mayer

So, with something like that as a launch event and a discussion about how this would look, we began our letter-writing campaign. Let me tell you, it went so much better than I could have hoped it would! The entire atmosphere of the class changed once the students started looking for the good in others. I think we can all agree how strange, and powerful, it is that when you go looking for something, you tend to find it. I had asked them to look for the good in others, which they did, and they certainly found it. As others found goodness in each one of them, their behaviors started to change too; they wanted something good to be found and that made them be better people and better classmates. It was one of my first forays into seeing how I could impact student behavior in unexpected and positive ways, and I now find this to be one of the most rewarding parts of teaching.

I'm telling you about the letter-writing now because if you have a toxic classroom environment, you will have to clean that up first so that you have some baseline of interpersonal functionality. It's only in a functional classroom environment that this grading structure I'm offering will work. Establishing norms with your students for their learning environment will be critical. If you are living with a set of classroom "rules" from Teachers Pay Teachers, cute as that poster may be, it is not likely something students are willing to hold each other accountable for. Use class time to have a serious discussion about what behaviors are acceptable in the classroom and why. Students should contribute meaningfully and sign off personally with their agreement once consensus is reached. Skipping this step is ill advised for creating a collegial classroom environment that will foster teamwork.

A Framework for Teamwork

Now, back to the teamwork experiment. Once you believe your classroom is at least a mildly positive environment, you are ready to embark on forming teams. As for me, it's a team for EVERYTHING. Ironically, helping students learn to be independent should begin with helping them learn to be good team players.

You have already read about how to construct a project that will be motivational, calling back to that Student-Choice Continuum graphic once again (which can be found in Chapter 8 if you want a quick refresher). Remember, there must be enough student choice so that the work is empowering, not just delegated. Ideally the work helps someone outside of the classroom and/or has an audience from outside the classroom; hopefully students are making a lot of choices and doing things in ways that are unique to them. Another aspect to consider is giving students specific jobs to work as their part of the team and holding them accountable for those jobs in particular. In addition to one's role as a team member, each person also has to contribute to the final output of the team, so this is just a description of the teamwork part of the job.

Here are some roles to consider:

- **Information Officer:** This person is responsible for being able to find all of the materials given to the team or collected throughout the project to form the final product. They must be able to answer any questions about content, requirements, and product the team needs to know.

- **Project Manager:** This person is responsible for the team's timeline and documenting each person's role in the project. What is each team member responsible for procuring or producing for the team? This person should know the answer and document all decisions made regarding this area. In addition, this person should form a project plan that includes when different parts of the assignment should be completed to stay on track and they should know where the team is on each part of the project at any given time.

- **Foray/Communications Manager:** This person is responsible for anything requiring leaving the classroom or communicating with other classes, teachers, community members, and so on. This person works with their team on those communications and makes sure that everyone agrees on what is needed and that communications that are being sent out are clear and correct. This person may also be responsible for asking questions for the team during Free Question Time or when the team decides to use a Question Slip.

- **Technology Coordinator:** This person is responsible for helping the team choose tools or achieve goals with technology. If technology is not working properly, this person may assist in solutions or communicate with school or personal resources to help solve problems. This team member may also work with the teacher to gather necessary tools or equipment the team needs in the area of technology.

- **Graphics and Marketing Coordinator:** A successful project looks the part and sells itself through consistent language, graphics, and other communication strategies. The person in this position helps craft a vision so that the team itself and others will better understand the project or product. The person in this role may make videos, flyers, or other materials to help "sell" the vision of the team to others.

Note: I loved having team roles and being able to call together all of the roles at once to give directions to them. This imbued them with a sense of importance and greatly increased their listening skills. If I'm introducing a new technology tool, I might do a 30-minute mini lesson that is only for those in the Technology Coordinator role. Think how seriously students will take this meeting when several other students are depending on them to bring back clear, correct information.

Journaling Activity

Take a moment to think about each of these job duties and answer the following questions in a journal entry:

- Which one of these jobs sounds the most fun or interesting to you?
- Have you taken on one of these roles in the past, even if it wasn't as clearly stated or defined?
- How do you think clearly defined job duties, such as these, may help to improve the group project experience for students?

You can, and should, play around with the job titles and descriptions to make them fit your classroom environment, grade level, and the type of project being completed. I found with high school students that I did not need to keep using these roles once students learned how to work cooperatively and collaboratively, and once the classroom climate and culture was positive; however, I was always prepared to return to them and a more stringent system of teamwork accountability should the need arise. I often kept the Technology Coordinator role even if I had not defined other roles because I found it much more effective to work with that small number of students and empower them than to try to work with the entire class on technical skills. With younger students, having roles addressing teamwork skills ongoing may be more important than with older students.

Creating and Evaluating Teamwork

Ultimately, the thing everyone hates about group projects, though, is the evaluation system. I spent several minutes today reading jokes on the internet and I decided to take a poll from my own team at friEdTech. It's probably no surprise that all these top performers whom I now work with every day were the "ones who did all the work" in every group project they ever participated in, and their chief complaint was other people essentially getting credit from their work. It just didn't feel fair; they either wanted the credit or at least didn't want anyone else taking credit they didn't deserve. This hits at a core human need that is ignored when we do not properly separate the parts of the project. As a reminder, those parts are: 1) the learning goals, 2) the product (output), and 3) the teamwork.

The learning goals are something you will address when you construct the project. You will probably use your school's curriculum to figure out what the product of the project will be. I would encourage you to think of it in this way: "If my students could produce ___, I would be sure they would know how to ___."

Examples	
If my students could create a great fictional, short film, script, or story . . .	I would be sure they understood the elements of plot and characterization.
If my students could create an animal and describe its ecosystem . . .	I would be sure they understood an animal's relationship to its ecosystem.
If my students could design and build a simple machine . . .	I would be sure they understood simple machines and how they work.
If my students could design a house with these parameters . . .	I would be sure they understood measuring the area of these shapes.

Something that is important to note: I would not advise you to teach the outcome before the project. For example, if your goal is for students to learn about plot and characterization by reading something together that has good plot and characterization, talk about it with them, but do not specifically teach these concepts. The learning will happen as students are actually doing the work. If you try to teach it, then have them do the work, it will be delegated and not empowered work, changing the whole energy of the project. Do not remove the element of the unknown and steal the learning; there are literally hundreds of ways for them to learn about these things, and it should not matter to you how they do it. Leave all the choices you can in the hands of the students.

Also important to note: I would be sure to create a different project scope for each team so that the team is responsible for teaching its part of the project to the rest of the class. This creates a need outside of just doing the work since each team will be responsible for teaching their classmates in other groups something; if there is another audience, even better, for example, other students, parents, administrators, and so on. You can either assign topics for each of the teams or create a system for them to choose for themselves. I always tried to make all of the topics interesting, and when I introduced them, I told the class what I thought was interesting about each one of them so that no one felt like they got the "bad" or "boring" topic, even if they didn't get their first choice. I learned that if I genuinely think something is interesting, it's easy to get other people interested in it. This was a very important part of building projects for me, that is, thinking of what would be really interesting about them for myself, and by extension, my students. Often I would run a project concurrently to reading a piece of literature. I might not address literature the same way today as I did then; I would probably give students many more choices and use reading groups so that there were many different books being read at the same time, but I didn't have the knowledge to do that at the time I was teaching, so we all read the same book at the same time.

Even though I am, by and large, giving you project ideas I used in my own classroom that might not be the subject you teach, I think having some general examples still makes constructing these projects easier to understand. So, I'll give you the details of one project my students and I really enjoyed. If you are not a literature teacher, or a secondary teacher, my hope is that you will still be able to apply the ideas behind these topics to your own grade level and subject area. With high school students, I used the edgiest topics I thought I could get away with in the community where

I taught. I wanted to build an interest in every conceivable way I could, staying just inside the line of administration and parent expectations. For the time, place, and audience I worked with, these topics worked, but I must acknowledge that they definitely would not fly in all communities.

I wanted my students to read the famous and award-winning book, later an Oscar-winning film, the first in 41 years to sweep the best picture, director, actor, and screenplay categories, *One Flew Over the Cuckoo's Nest*. The book was fascinating, well written, had an interesting historical context, and I loved the aspect of learning about the historical context of the book for my students who were, for the most part, not getting a stellar education in history. It was a time they often didn't even "get to" in history class but a time that would usually be of high interest to teenagers with all of the drama, rebellion, and political unrest. The following is a summary of the unit plan I used for this project.

One Flew Over the Cuckoo's Nest Unit Plan

"The answer is never the answer. What's really interesting is the mystery. If you seek the mystery instead of the answer, you'll always be seeking. I've never seen anybody really find the answer—they think they have, so they stop thinking. But the job is to seek mystery, evoke mystery, plant a garden in which strange plants grow and mysteries bloom. The need for mystery is greater than the need for an answer." —Ken Kesey

Reading Schedule *One Flew Over the Cuckoo's Nest*
3/27 pages 9–18, **3/28** pages 19–41, **4/1** pages 42–68, **4/2** pages 69–91, **4/4** pages 92–115, **4/7** pages 116–137, **4/9** pages

138–162, **4/11** pages 163–190, **4/14** pages 191–218, **4/16** pages 219–241.

Project and Grading

One Flew Over the Cuckoo's Nest is a strange and controversial book written in a strange and controversial time by a strange and controversial man. Your job is to take each of the following mysterious topics and work with your team to provide an explanation and background for your class and our audience. Your team will have up to 15 minutes to present the most interesting and relevant information about your topic in whatever way you devise to be the most effective, memorable, and educational.

Ms. Mayer will grade your team using the rubric attached. Her score will count for 80% of your team's grade. Your class and audience (which may consist of: administrators, teachers, and other students) will also score your team and provide the other 20% of the project's grade. In addition, you will be graded by and have an opportunity to grade your teammates' contributions to the projects as usual. Here is a sample grade for a fictional student named Joe:

- Ms. Mayer gives Joe's team a 94 on its project and presentation. This part of the project comprises 80% of the team's grade and is the same for everyone on the team.

- Joe's team's audience gives his project an average score of 96. This part of the project comprises 20% of the team's grade and is the same for everyone on the team.

- Joe's teammates give him an 82, 92, and 80, and Joe gives himself a 100; the average of Joe's team evaluations is 88.5% . This part of the project determines Joe's percentage of the earnings from the team's grade.

Here's Joe's grade:

Ms. Mayer's grade of the product/output of the team:

$$94 \times 80\% = +75.2 \text{ points}$$

Audience Average score of the product/output of the team:

$$96 \times 20\% = +19.2 \text{ points}$$

Team's Grade:

$$94.4 \text{ points} (75.2 + 19.2)$$

Average of Joe's teammates' scores for his contributions to this project: (82, 92, 80, 100), meaning the average score for Joe is 88.5

Joe is eligible for 88.5% of the grade his team earned together on this project. Therefore, Joe's grade is:

$.885 \times 94.4$, which equals 83.54 or 84 points, rounded up

This is a competitive project, which means at least one team's product will make a score of 100.

The following is a list of the topics for our class. You may choose your topic by writing your name and desired topic on a scrap of paper, which will place you in a team. If more than five students vote for a topic, Ms. Mayer will meet with the teams to help decide who gets which topic.

You may also propose your own topic, and we will do our best to form a team around it.

- Biography of Ken Kesey
- Biography of Timothy Leary
- Biography of Jack Kerouac
- Film *One Flew Over the Cuckoo's Nest*

- Merry Pranksters
- Counterculture
- History of electroshock therapy and current uses
- History of the lobotomy procedure and contrast current treatments and philosophies
- Staff Interviews: Lois Buckman, Elizabeth Blevins, Toni Hill (Note: I love this part of the project! These were real staff members from the school where I taught who had significant experiences during the time we were studying. They loved participating in the project and the students had such fun interviewing them and researching the historical events in which they had participated. Lois, Elizabeth, and Toni, thank you for being there for us and sharing your experiences!)

That is the project summary I would have given to my students. I don't remember for sure, but I would imagine I gave it to them toward the end of a class period to give them time to do some preliminary research and mull over the list of potential topics. This was not the first project they did with me, so they would have had some ideas how they wanted to do things differently. If I were concerned about the teams, I would not have given students time to plan topics outside of class. In this particular class where we executed this project, the interpersonal dynamics were very good.

The two parts of the project that you will be evaluating as the teacher are the output (product) that the students create and the way the team works together to accomplish that output (teamwork). Both of these parts of the project are extremely important and both are fully in the hands of the students. But how you describe and design them will determine whether you build or kill the motivation you want your students to experience. As far as the product of the student teams goes, I always liked to encourage creativity and competition, which is why I announced up front that at least one team would make a 100. NOW, for an individual student to achieve a 100, they had to ALSO get a 100 for the peer audience AND from their teammates, which is extremely hard to do, but you could emerge from this project with a 100, in theory.

What studies have found is that if you know you can pay your bills and live your life, the amount of money you make beyond that doesn't contribute much to your happiness. So even if you win the mega millions lottery, you won't be happy unless you already are, unless that win takes you out of a life of poverty. Strangely, grades seem to work the same way except that where I taught, there were a significant number of students who just didn't care about grades at all. For those students who did care, these things were important and could not be overlooked. I wanted to build in so much motivation in so many different ways that there was something that was going to hook in each one of my students, so I did not want to miss any opportunities.

Please note: grades do not come out of your paycheck, so if they motivate your students, use them! For those students who cared about grades, knowing they could earn a 100 was awesome! For those who did not care about grades, I had peers evaluating each other, that score would likely be more meaningful to them. No one wants to let down their teammates or be seen as irresponsible, irrelevant, or as a noncontributor. In spite of the fact that we have all worked together in teams where people behave like they don't care, putting a number on it and giving an opportunity for peers to actually evaluate sweeps that lie aside. EVERYONE CARES, outside of an extremely small percentage of people, and I taught none of those rare individuals, at least not that I know of.

Regarding the products (or outcomes), of course, it was important that students were researching, discussing, reading, writing, and creating: all of that was very important. Because they knew their peers would be seeing and judging their presentations, this built in a tremendous amount of intrinsic care for the output of the work. To quote Kevin Honecutt's song from a previous chapter, "I Want My Teacher to Learn" (you can find it on YouTube; it always makes me cry!), "An audience of one, well, it's so absurd." If what your students are working on is not even important enough for YOU to look at it, imagine the absurdly small amount of time and attention THEY feel like giving it if they don't care about grades. I don't have a scale that can weigh that amount of care because it's less than zero grams.

In contrast to how things were before, with that scale measuring less than zero grams of care for my assignments, after I started teaching this way, my students often did not even want to tell me what they were planning to show until the day final products were revealed, which I have to admit was both scary and fun. One day I arrived at the door of my classroom before first period to find my room was already full of students, some in costume, and every one with a name tag on. The tags put each of the students, and me, into a social strata, either Royal (only me...I got to be the queen!), Middle Class (only a few students qualified for this group), and peasants, which was a large (scientifically large, it turns out) group. The team that set all of this up was responsible for showing us what social structures were like in Shakespeare's society. Up to this point, I had no idea how they were planning to do this or that they were getting to school 30 minutes early or that we would be having a full-fledged dinner at 7:30 in the morning, but that's what they did. Mr. Kenny, our school janitor, had let them into the room to set up more than half an hour before I even got to campus. It was both a little scary (I had no idea any of it was happening) and extremely rewarding (they knocked it out of the park with a demonstration that no one involved will probably ever forget).

Each of us only got to eat from the foods designated for our social strata. The peasants got "gruel," which they had reproduced with pea soup and a few, scarce chunks of ham. (They even heated it up.) The small middle class had many more options of foods to consume and there was some decorative quality to the presentation of this food. During this time in history, the middle class was a new and rising group. Finally, there was me, the Queen of the demonstration. I had a beautiful arrangement and variety that was exclusively available to me. It was pretty amazing to hear the conversations among students who were so annoyed they only qualified for peasant food and to hear how unfair they found this situation. I wonder how those peasants in real life felt if they felt this way about a free breakfast they didn't even know they were getting? Once we were all seated with our designated foods, the presentation began and we learned about life in a different time. After my students produced this project, I worried less, at least in this class, about whether they would take their jobs seriously.

What follows is the explanation I gave my students before we ever started the first team or group project about how they would be graded on group participation. For me, it was another total game-changer. I entered the discussion seriously, like I was talking to employees about a salary structure, and my students responded with similar gravity and asked good questions that let me know they were listening and valued the effort I put into making our classroom a place to contribute that might be more fair than any one they had experienced before.

Group Work without the Group Grade

To avoid the problems with "group grades," each group member will evaluate him/herself, as well as every other group participant, as follows:

Example Evaluation:

Team Member Name: Sally

Percentage team member completed of project: 20%

Percentage of the grade you think the team member should be eligible for: 80%

Did the team member participate equally? Not really. Sally goofed off ½ a period one day.

Justify the percentage of the grade you awarded:
That day Sally goofed off and she made us miss a deadline on part of our project. She said she was going to the bathroom, but she was really talking to her boyfriend in the hallway. But the rest of the time she worked hard. Still, she didn't give 100% like everyone else did.

Let's say Sally's other team members give her a 75, an 85, and she gives herself a 100.

80

75

85

<u>100</u>

85 Sally's average evaluation is 85%.

If the teacher awards the team a 92 on the project, here's how we figure out Sally's initial grade:

Teacher's grade = 92 × .85 (percentage Sally earned) = Sally's grade: 78

This is called the "initial grade" because if Sally doesn't agree with the percentage her team members say she earned, she is free to have a conference with the teacher privately and provide evidence of her contributions. In this case, since Sally's team members evaluated her so similarly, the teacher can feel pretty confident that 85% accurately reflects her contribution to the team.

The teacher will never share individual team members' evaluations of other team members; however, any student can discuss their average with Ms. Mayer and ask for a recalculation.

On the day of team evaluations, I would use the gradebook's seating chart feature or a spreadsheet to create a quick seating chart where no one would be sitting near anyone they worked with on the project being evaluated. This chart was just temporary, so there wouldn't be much complaining about it. We took team evaluations VERY seriously in my classroom. Each student would receive a printout of the Team Evaluation form like the following one.

This project grading strategy was passed on to me by a friend and colleague, Dean Frederick, who was a math teacher at The Woodlands College Park High School at the time he told me about the idea. I adapted it, but as Dean reported, it turned out to be a highly effective way of looking at team contribution. The real magic of it is that it separates the content/product/output of the team from the teamwork, and that is critical for some reason to our psychological needs.

So what you are probably wondering now is what do real students do in real life when faced with this situation? I wondered that too and I consistently found the results interesting every time I used this strategy. First of all, I wanted to take all the time they wanted to understand this new process before the first project ever started. Most students didn't have many questions about it, but it allayed the fears of those who had been in project hell with other teachers and students; I guess it gave them the idea that I at least knew how dreaded "group work" normally went and had some idea that the system needed to be repaired. Once the first project of the year began with these guidelines in place—this was after we had practiced various smaller, shorter-term ventures where we learned to rely on and get along with each other—I heard some very interesting conversations around the classroom.

With this way of teaching, I was no longer relegated to constantly correcting my students. I was able to be that mythic "guide on the side" we've all been hearing fables about for the last 10 years. Even when I was seated working on something at my desk, I could hear the energetic conversations going on around me, and sometimes that was

Name of Evaluator: _____

Team Evaluation: _____ project _____

(name of project)

Self-Evaluation (Team Member One, YOU!):
Percentage team member completed of project: (25% ideal for four member team, 20% for five member team)
Percentage of the grade you think the team member should be eligible for: (usually 80–100%)
Did the team member participate equally?
Justify the percentage of the grade you awarded:
Team Member Two Name:
Percentage team member completed of project:
Percentage of the grade you think the team member should be eligible for:
Did the team member participate equally?
Justify the percentage of the grade you awarded:
Team Member Three Name:
Percentage team member completed of project:
Percentage of the grade you think the team member should be eligible for:
Did the team member participate equally?

Justify the percentage of the grade you awarded:
Team Member Four Name:
Percentage team member completed of project:
Percentage of the grade you think the team member should be eligible for:
Did the team member participate equally?
Justify the percentage of the grade you awarded:
Team Member Five Name:
Percentage team member completed of project:
Percentage of the grade you think the team member should be eligible for:
Did the team member participate equally?
Justify the percentage of the grade you awarded:

the best place to sit, listen, and really understand what was going on in the groups. I often observed while doing something else because I didn't want to affect what was going on inside a team unless there was a reason to, such as offering a guiding question or responding to a Question Slip. As far as how these grading guidelines impacted student behavior, there was no doubt in my mind that the change in behavior in my classroom was a direct result of this new process. I heard people say things like, "Jimmy, you have to remember to bring that work tomorrow like you said you would or I'm gonna mark you down, like, seriously. We're off track and we need it. Okay?" Or, "I want y'all to remember I'm doing this when you're grading me, okay! This wasn't my part and I'm doing it now. Everybody is going to remember this, right?!" Not only were they evaluating each other very closely, but they began championing their own, as well as each other's, efforts in the project, which is another critical skill to learn (we all have to brag on ourselves sometimes or at least know our contributions are seen).

Did teams ever get the team grading wrong? I can honestly say no, I don't ever remember one instance where a whole team got the grade wrong. However, to anyone who has taught in a classroom, I'm sure it is no surprise that with the interpersonal relationships at work, there were times where one score would be totally out of line with the rest. For example, if Joe's team gave him these scores: 82, 92, 30, 100, I would do two things. First, I would check the other scores team member three gave to the rest of the group. If they were all in this range, I would ask them, individually, to talk to me about why they were so low. It could be they misunderstood and thought the percentage of the work (usually 25%) was the same as the percentage of the grade (hopefully 100%). If Team Member 3 ONLY gave Joe the low grade and there wasn't any explanation that made this make sense, I would silently discard that 30%.

Before: 82, 92, 30, 100, average 76, which would have made Joe's grade 76% of 94.4, which is 72.

After: 82, 92, 100, average 91, which makes Joe's grade 91% of 94.4, which is instead 86.

I would speak to neither Joe nor Team Member 3 about this change. The 30% is so far out of range with the rest of the scores AND there was no justification. If multiple team members gave Joe such low scores, then I would know he really didn't contribute adequately over a long period of time. I always gave every student the right to appeal their grade but they could ONLY know the average score their team gave them and they only had ONE of those numbers at their disposal, the score they gave themselves.

As I've spoken about this grading method over the years, many teachers have asked me if all students give themselves a 100%, and my answer usually surprises the person asking. NO, almost no student gave themselves a 100. Most often, the score students give themselves is in line with the scores their peers give them. The truth is, most of us know how we've contributed to a team and when we know our scores are being compared with others who also know, I guess this improves our honesty quotient, reinforcing that critical skill of self-evaluation. There were always students who felt they deserved a 100 on everything, but even those students usually did not give themselves a 100 on this assignment unless they were really sure they had been a fantastic teammate, and could prove that empirically.

Another question I've gotten before is about what happens if students give themselves or others over 100%. Let's say Joe turned out to be the MVP of the group. His team gave him these scores: 95, 110, 105, and he gave himself a 100. His average then is 104%. I gave the team a 94.4, so Joe's grade would be 98 (94.4 × 104%, or 98%). Is this okay with me as the teacher? Absolutely! My goal with this part of the project is to teach people to work together productively and produce motivation for our learning environment. Do I really think Joe learned this much more than the rest of his team? Almost certainly not, BUT did he put in that much more time and effort? Could be. Remember: as teachers, grades don't come out of our paychecks, and I'm not in charge of rationing points in this evaluation model. My job is to create an environment where students are learning and feeling part of a community.

Importantly, during each of these projects we did every year, there were plenty of checkpoints, quizzes, tests, and other measures that were focused on individual performance. It's not that I don't believe individual performance is relevant or important; it certainly is, but I know that when people work together to learn new things, powerful forces come into play that can never be produced *without* collaboration, and these forces help each of us to achieve as individuals as well as inside our teams. I also don't think it's too far-fetched to say that structuring a classroom like this is good for students' mental health and well-being. Unfortunately, many students go through their schooling feeling extremely isolated and disconnected from others. In a learning community like ours, it was not possible for someone to be completely excluded socially. Even students who were on the autism spectrum or who had learning disabilities were able to connect and contribute meaningfully with their peers, which was extremely rewarding to see and sometimes an experience they never had in school before.

Reflection Activity

What do you think about this method of evaluation? Think of a group project you have worked on in the past, either in school or at work. Take a few moments to reflect on this chapter through the lens of that project, using the following questions as a guide.

- Was the work split equally?

- Even if it was split up equally, did everyone apply the same amount of effort to the project?

- If this modality of evaluation had been used, how do you think that may have affected how the team worked together or the outcome itself?

- How would an evaluation system like this have changed your own "group work" experience?

Takeaways

1. There are aspects of human psychology, like the need to feel one is treated fairly, that are often not taken into account during schooling experiences. Considering our own needs and examining our own experiences can lead us to design better learning environments and learning experiences than the ones we were a part of during our own schooling.

2. When students are working in groups or teams, the learning goals, the product (output), and the team-work should be viewed and evaluated separately, and

individuals should be assessed individually on the learning outcomes.

3. Creating an environment that fosters teamwork gives students opportunities to become a part of a learning community that some will not experience without a teacher like you who understands the value of this important work and chooses to get beyond the worksheet.

Is Artificial Intelligence a Worksheet Killer?

A spokesman for Seattle Public Schools was quoted in the *New York Times* naming ChatGPT, released in November 2022, as one of "five cheating tools" the district had banned. A "cheating tool,"[1] wait, what? There's an old adage that if the only tool you have is a hammer, every problem is a nail, and that could be the clearest explanation of how an artificial intelligence (AI) engine got swiftly reduced by many educators and educational institutions as "a cheating tool." When I was in the 3rd grade, a handheld calculator was viewed in about the same way, with a similar amount of disdain. Lucky for me, I had an innovative 4th-grade math teacher. I'd fallen out of the "high" (honors) math class the year before when I could not, or would not, memorize the times tables at the required rate of speed in order to stay in the class. Honestly, I just hated the math worksheets so much that I couldn't make myself do them. I still remember the shame of the situation and I know for sure that being relegated to the "regular" class for math set me up for a lifetime of feeling "not good" at math and generally just having all kinds of icky experiences and feelings associated with numbers. Honestly, I just never could make myself care about numbers the way I did, and still do, about words. I learned in the last few years that people other than myself have all kinds of associations, ideas, and feelings about numbers and patterns of numbers. For the most part, they might as well be random ancient runes as far as my brain is concerned. Was it 500,000 or 5,000,000? Unless there is a dollar sign there and you tell me it's my bank balance, I won't be able to tell you later which one . . . maybe it was just 5,000 or was it three-something instead? I will be unlikely to know since I am unable to hold onto the significance of them in my brain. I used to think there was something wrong with me, and as a child, I was certain there had to be. I thought I was lazy where math was concerned and there might be some truth to that if I'm being honest. The longer I live, though, the more I think that if I had been taught using math instruction methods that are in place now I might have had more "number sense" that might have led to greater success in my math experiences, starting with that "cheating tool," the calculator.

I thought my math problems were over for one day in 4th grade when my teacher, Mrs. McClendon, brought out the new and magical handheld calculator. There was also, obviously, a worksheet involved, but this time, we used the calculator to key in the problems and get the answers; not very sophisticated, I know, but stay with me here. The fact that anyone even put a calculator in front of 10-year-olds inside a school building was astonishing and borderline revolutionary at the time. I know that, even then, even with this very minor technology, the decision was not free from controversy. The calculator was a huge and polarizing topic of discussion in education, raising questions from "Will students still need math education if they have calculators" to "How will we ever know if people can 'do' math if these things are everywhere?" and I'm sure so many more worries and fears. The thing I remember most was that using the calculator was a one-time anomaly, and I was very displeased with returning to head-based (read as *impossible* for me) minor calculations. Someone in the class asked why, with the school owning the calculators (obviously) and us having access to them (they were *RIGHT THERE* on the shelf) we didn't just use them all the time in class. The answer was resounding and certain, "You won't always have access to calculators, so you have to be able to do math quickly in your head." Cue the sad trombone because that ship had sailed for me back in 3rd grade; I was never going to be "good" at what these folks called math without a calculator.

I wish I could call up Mrs. McClendon now and resume the argument if she would take up the other side, which I doubt. I *AM TOO* always going to have a "calculator" with me—it's right there inside my smartphone to which I am unfortunately tethered at all times. "*CAN TOO, CAN TOO, CAN TOO!*" my inner elementary student wants to shout. But, that's not the way the world of schooling works; just because the "outside" world changes (calculators are made small, cheap, and therefore, ubiquitous, and then integrated into cell phones) doesn't mean the world inside of a school must change at all. Since no one I knew had a calculator at home, the school rescinding the privilege of using the thing was all it took to make the tool go completely away for many years. Oh, but we hadn't even conceived of the internet and the way it would, theoretically, upend every-thing. Mrs. McClendon, you just wait.

At some point, I guess the calculator discussion cleared up and someone, somewhere decided that, for some reason, only people who already were pretty good at math could use them, and then only for things that were deemed very hard to do without a calculator, and even THEN only in ways that would be beyond the understanding of a nor-mal 4th grader like myself. When my daughter was in high school, we were required to provide a model of the Texas Instruments calculator for her advanced math class; I think it was a TI-89. It cost around $100 and was certainly not something that most folks would want to carry in their pock-ets or purses, but it was deemed necessary and we ponied up the cash for it. Our less studious son made it all the way through his K–12 schooling career without ever needing the thing. I don't know if that's because he didn't care enough to bring home the request (likely) or if he didn't attain the level of math his sister did (also likely), but either way, no TI—whatever number—was required.

My point is that eventually, the calculator made its way into the education system as a staple, just not in the way anyone probably originally thought it would. As far as I am aware, most students are still memorizing times tables and this is still considered foundational math knowledge that must be memorized by everyone, so, I would still probably have the same sticking point even if I got an elementary school mulligan. Would the modern math instruction focus-ing more on logical and reasonable thinking have saved me from the middle-earth math class? Maybe, possibly, but not entirely likely. The bigger issue might be in the leveling like this of instruction at all, but I digress. We're here to talk about how technological innovation in the "outside world" gets transmuted inside the world of education.

Calculators, the Internet, and ChatGPT

So, what happens when there is a technological innovation like the calculator, the internet, or ChatGPT? What does the monolith of public education do to accommodate? Hand-held calculators, personal computers, smartphones, and AI, like ChatGPT, are all good examples of innovations that have already or will soon vastly change the way we do business and even what knowledge or skills are considered valuable. For example, the value of the ability to do math problems in your head decreased when everyone had quick, easy access to the calculator in our phones. It became more important and valuable to understand when a result or "answer" was logical or reasonable than to be able to actually do the individual calculations. When the personal computer became a household item, schools only had a few machines available for any type of student use, but only if you signed up for a specific class that "needed" them. When I was in high school, there were only computers in one classroom, the "business" room where we went to attend business specialized classes; meanwhile years earlier, in France, people were already using the Minitel system to look up phone numbers from home. By 1986, my freshman year of high school, 1.4 million terminals were connected to Minitel, and newspapers were worried the technology would put them out of business, though their stated opposition was that the Minitel would "separate people from each other and endanger social relationships."[2] I wonder how many times and over how many years that argument has been made? Surely Gutenberg himself must have heard it when the printing press came into fashion. Unlike the country of France, where people were using a type of internet before *the* internet even existed, my high school had three computers by 1989, the beginning of my senior year. I don't think anyone knew what to do with them; much like the one day's use of calculators, they were seen as a bit of a nuisance as much as they were also a novelty. You could barely get them to do any of the things they were supposed to do, and what they were even intended to do was hard to discern the benefit of. As a word processor, they were only superior if you could make the darn things print, and that was an entirely separate issue. Since you couldn't send anyone anything digitally, unless the step of printing was achieved, and printing also required special paper with holes properly spaced for the dot matrix printer to grab onto, you weren't doing anything with that computer you weren't going to go at again on a typewriter later. One hall over was Mrs. Braziel's room where we learned to type on "real" typewriters, electric ones. The path to the printed word was certain there; you could literally see the printing happening while you were doing the process. It seemed quite a bit better to me in comparison, but only if you knew what you were going to say. No one cared what any of us had to say. We were meant to type in what our bosses told us, so that wasn't much of an issue.

My sophomore year of high school I had a wonderful counselor who really encouraged me. She went so far out of her way, taking a special interest in me, nominating me for the Hugh O'Brian Youth Leadership award and even taking me to Houston, the nearest big city, to compete and meet other students who had won this award. It was a really big deal for a small-town girl like me who hadn't gotten out much. I truly wish I could thank her now. Sadly, she died of a sudden, aggressive cancer before the end of the very same school year. Her replacement was less impressive; I remember that she was elderly, though to me at the time, 50 probably equated to one foot in the grave, but I genuinely think she must have been in her 70s and not the young, vibrant sort of 70 we often see today. This lady had a polyester suit and knew how to get long wear out of it. I think I remember there being the standard pantyhose and heels every day, and I know there was a head of gray hair in a helmet-like disposition. This "new" counselor fill-in wasn't impressed with me either, not one bit. She sat me down for a mandatory "what are you going to do with your life" meeting and within 30 minutes declared that if I "worked hard" (I was in honors classes and made all As and Bs), I could be an executive secretary or even a court reporter, though it was implied the latter was a fair stretch based on what was sitting in her office in that moment. I was, and still am, offended by the accusation that those jobs were all I was cut out for. Both of them were tied to typing other people's words and not my own. I hold plenty of respect for both of those professions, truly, but no one wants to be told at 16 years old that the best that they can hope for is to work for somebody else for the rest of their lives, even though almost every single one of us will. At 16, we should all want to be entrepreneurs or presidents and we shouldn't be told that we cannot achieve those lofty goals. As a teacher, I learned it was much better to let life teach them instead.

In 1988, knowledge work wasn't a thing, or if it was, we didn't know about it yet. If you said you were going to be "an artist," people would just laugh at you. Maybe they still do, but there are hundreds of ways to be a working, well-paid artist now; no one could think of any other one but being Picasso back then. And, there were only a few career paths that were acceptable for women from my part of the world, so my fill-in counselor's advice wasn't actually that bad in that regard. I had already been told my entire life that I was going to college though, so I was annoyed that this ancient woman was implying that I wasn't cut out for that path. Obviously, I didn't let her limited expectations stop me. I had my one day in the sun with the calculator and figured there might be more on the horizon, and while I had excelled in typing class, that was little more than a game to me. I figured someone else would be typing for me later on, maybe even somebody like her (ha!).

Change in the Outside World versus Change Inside Educational Systems

I think most of us know that new technologies can take a long time to work their way into schools, if they ever do at all. During my K–12 schooling career, the calculator and the personal computer are the only two I can think of that did well enough to make an eventual appearance. Looking at schools today with millions upon millions of Chromebooks, iPads, and other form factors of devices, you might think massive changes have occurred, and in some ways, you would be right, but in other ways, not so much. As exemplified by the calculator story, a school owning a technology does not equate to it using that technology in any sort of meaningful, relevant, or impactful way, if it is being used at all. We "used" the calculator, one day, for one task (simple math problems we all already could do without the calculator), and we used the computer as a typewriter, nothing more. Neither of these technologies changed my education meaningfully.

The same can be said for many children's educations today in spite of the utter and inarguable ubiquity of the portable technology that is available to us today. I met up with one of my former high school students a few years ago and had an interesting discussion about this topic. She is now a Scrum Master for an oil and gas company, works in a high-stress environment, and is well compensated for her considerable skills and abilities. It was so interesting to hear about how she leverages technology in her day-to-day work. When the topic turned to her own children, both of whom were preschool aged at the time, she asked some interesting questions about what I was doing in this field of education technology. The conversation went something like this: "Mrs. Mayer, what does that even mean? No one uses paper anymore, so do you just show teachers how to collaborate with the computer or what? Like, what part of it is it that they don't know yet?" After a few minutes of conversation, I learned that Jenny thought that in the years since she graduated from high school, the entire world of education had transformed, just as HER world had transformed, into a paperless environment where every child of every age interacted with computerized devices of one variety or another and teacher communications, similarly, were all done online.

I was so flabbergasted by her misunderstanding; it took me a long time to catch up to what she was laying down. I had to let her know that since she'd left my classroom for the last time, virtually *nothing* had changed except that the computers were smaller and easier to carry around. Most assignments were still done with pencil and paper; if they were done on a computer, they were generally still printed out to then be turned in to a physical inbox. Little kids rarely used any technology in school other than for a few learning games. In the district her children now attend, they probably touch a computer-based device a few times a week, if that. Their "Wednesday Folders" will still be filled with the

Journaling Activity

I want you to think of a piece of technology (hardware or software) that you have either used in the classroom or that you would like to see used in the classroom in the future. With this tool in mind, ask yourself the following questions:

- What type of reaction did you see, or would you expect to receive, from your students, fellow teachers, and administrators if/when this tool was used in your classroom?

- Were any of the reactions you saw, or those that you would expect to see, negative? If so, why do you think that might be? If not, what did you do, or plan to do, ahead of the implementation that supported the tool's reception?

- If this tool was being used to its fullest potential, how could it transform your, and other, classrooms?

Is Artificial Intelligence a Worksheet Killer?   **227**

same types of paperwork her very own little "Wednesday Folder" was replete with all of those years ago. Let me tell you, she was absolutely shocked. This was so interesting to me, but I have continued to find that people outside of the education world have no idea what it takes to actually change a system and beyond that, how little impact a new technology can have on a thing that is so entrenched as an education system. Technology is much more likely to be used to accomplish a task like attempting to entertain or test someone than it is for the job of learning itself, and it still is rarely used in the way I want it to be, much as in my schooling career, neither the calculator nor the computer made any substantial change.

The Learning Path

The missing piece in this puzzle of technology implementation comes from a fundamental lack of understanding of how people learn, which has been exacerbated by the monster that is standardized testing. Earlier in this book I reminded you, and myself, of times when we used textbooks over our heads for bomb shelters thinking that would somehow protect us from some kind of nuclear fallout. Of course, that's silly, but it still happened. Those magically protective textbooks, along with many worksheets, were the foundation of my early education; they were literally all we had. They were the only thing between us and the "communists" seeking to destroy us. That sort of thinking, that learning is just about consumption and regurgitation, is the fundamental misunderstanding that still holds back the entire learning system from moving forward at more than a snail's pace (even though the technology we are seeing should be allowing us to take HUGE leaps forward in this space).

Learning, for most of us and for most things, just doesn't work the way we were always told that it did. You can't just hear something or read something and fully understand it, no matter how lucid the writing may be. You actually have to mess around with it, get things wrong, form and reform the thing you're seeking to understand to truly grasp the concept beyond memorizing facts. You have to see many examples of a thing, view it from a lot of angles, ask a lot of questions, get answers, argue with them, be wrong, then try again. You need a lot of stories, hopefully like the ones in this book, to really wrap your mind around something new. It's less like Figure 11.1

And more like Figure 11.2.

What we know now about learning is that it's a messy, nonlinear (at times seemingly nonsensical) process full of mistakes, false starts, and misunderstandings, and that's a good thing! It's only through a number of attempts and experiences that we can integrate new knowledge into old, and we only know if we actually "know" a thing when we can do something with the information we say we have integrated beyond regurgitate words. If, for example, we say we understand how to construct a meaningful sentence,

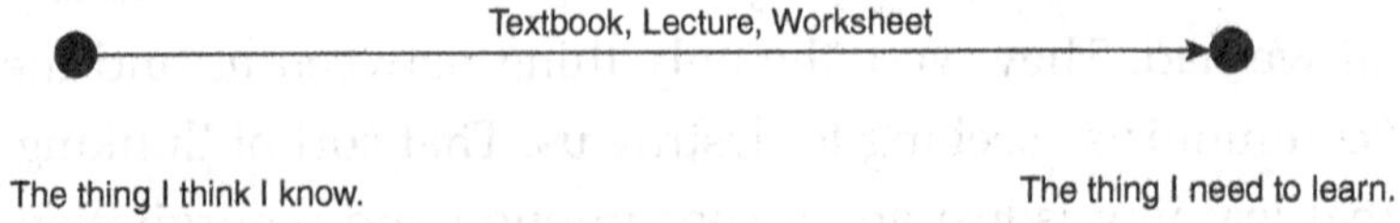

●————————— Textbook, Lecture, Worksheet —————————▶●

The thing I think I know.   The thing I need to learn.

FIGURE 11.1 Linear model of learning.

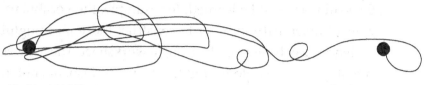

The thing I think I know.   The thing I need to learn.

FIGURE 11.2 Actual model of learning.

reading a prefabricated one aloud is not a test of that skill. Instead, we must be able to do the thing (create a new meaningful sentence, ideally about something that is meaningful to us), multiple times, and create meaning others can take away from our attempts. The meaning we're attempting to impart must be conveyed to the reader with a minimum of mistakes in translation, from our brain, to our writing medium, to the other person's reading medium, and into their thoughts. Unless I can reliably do that, I haven't mastered the skill at all. We can fine-tune the skill over years and years and get to a level of skill initially unimaginable, but only if we keep trying, failing, receiving feedback, and then trying again. However, simply reading (consuming written information) will never fully get us there. It's the recursive action of practice and feedback that leads to more practice that will help us achieve the goal of improving our ability to communicate what's in our minds and relay that information to another person's thoughts. All skills we're attempting to help students develop in school work in similar ways. Some of them can be broken down into discrete units more easily than others, but they all should be working toward some goal that ends up in the ability to do something of value that is far too complex and nuanced for a worksheet. The argument arises about whether the discrete parts of the skill that must be learned, for example, the vocabulary words I must learn in order to construct those meaningful sentences, can be learned by using a worksheet. The answer is that, yes, they could be, but the answer is also, no, not in the best way.

Let's use the topic of vocabulary development, which is important in every subject we study both in school and out, as an example. Vocabulary knowledge, much like those awful math facts from 3rd grade that still haunt me, is essential. The ability to pull up a word when one needs it, even with the advent and ubiquity of computers, is a consistently valuable skill. When I was a child who couldn't determine whether a calculation was mis-keyed or not, calculators had limited value to me. If I can't explain my point to my AI tool of choice well enough for its extraordinary computer brain to understand my goal, it also will not be able to write my essay, help me brainstorm additional ideas, or add any real value at all to my learning process or even to the output I seek to create. This skill of talking to AI already has a name; it's called Prompt Engineering, though I've read that AI will also make this skill set obsolete in the near future.

Maybe those of you who are modern math teachers were reading about my one glorious day of calculator use and thinking what a missed opportunity to teach WITH the technology that day was. The worksheet was the same old type of worksheet with math facts from the day before and the same old type of thing used the day after. The missed opportunity didn't have anything to do with the technology; it had to do with the understanding of the teacher about how technology would, or could, impact learning. I certainly don't blame Mrs. McClendon for the oversight!

Forty-some-odd years later most educators still don't understand how to make technology a part of learning in an effective manner. Instead we err in one of two ways; 1) we use technology as an entertainer/babysitter, or 2) technology is a direct replacement of something we were already doing on paper. The place we're trying, still, to get to is a place where we understand the technology, see its likely impact on the world, and learn how to leverage it to its highest potential, whether that's solving a problem we have, helping us overcome a disability, sharing our work with a profoundly larger audience, contributing to the world's body of knowledge, or simply replacing us by doing a task we find boring, repetitive, etc. The work that must be done to further incorporate technology into our classrooms is incredibly important, and we have data to support this claim. The Center for Applied Research in Educational Technology (CARET) found that, when used in conjunction with collaborative learning methods and coordinated with leadership that is aimed at improving the school through technology planning, technology impacts achievement in content area learning, promotes higher-order thinking and problem-solving skills, and prepares students for the workforce.[3]

In the case of ChatGPT, Gemini and other similar AI tools that have already become ubiquitous, there are so many tools that pretending to live in a world where tools in this category don't exist makes no more sense than using those calculators for one day only to do math facts we were expected to do the day before and the day after using our little noggins only. By reducing technology tools to the category of "cheating," we dismiss the amazing advancements in technology represented. We, as educators, should be embracing new tech and helping students figure out how it will impact their lives, how it may be used in their future careers, which assignments just became meaningless because of the technology, and which new ways of thinking will be required because of the technology.

Where ChatGPT and tools like it are concerned, most of the conversations I'm hearing inside our systems revolve around plagiarism. For example, a friend of mine, Heather Lewis Sanders, asked ChatGPT to "compose a speech lauding the Oxford comma in the style of Eminem." This is what it produced:

> Yo, listen up y'all, I got a story to tell
> About a comma that's small, but it packs a hell of a spell
> It's the Oxford comma, and some folks don't know
> But let me break it down, so you can flow with the flow
> See, it separates items in a list, it's real simple
> But when you leave it out, it can cause a rumple
> Like "I dedicate this to my parents, Beyoncé and Jay-Z"
> See how that could be misunderstood, it's crazy
> But with the Oxford comma in place, it's crystal clear
> "I dedicate this to my parents, Beyoncé, and Jay-Z"
> No confusion, no debate, it's what we need to state
> So listen up all you writers, and listen up all you readers
> The Oxford comma is a game changer, a real life saver
> Don't be lazy, don't be slack, use it in your sentences back
> And you'll be sure to avoid any confusion or attack

So remember, the Oxford comma is key
It's the difference between being understood
and being a D
So use it, and use it right, and you'll be winning
this fight
So that's it folks, I'm out, peace and love to y'all
And remember, the Oxford comma, it stands tall.

How cool is that?! Imagine how students could explore content that might not interest them in new ways that would make the content much more interesting to them. There are so many good questions to ask about this technology to get students, and ourselves, thinking about how it changes things. In order to evaluate this sample, we have to understand the Oxford comma and accompanying controversy and the style of Eminem. I understand the first, but some of you will have to be the judge on the latter topic. For me, the ability of a computer to do this type of work was unthinkable just a few months ago, and that makes it rather shocking. If I were still teaching writing, I would want my students to know about this tool and to try it and study the results. I would want them to think of how they could use it to their advantage, and I would want us to consider what new skills they were going to need to learn to address the use of the technology. What I would not want would be for my school district to label ChatGPT a "cheating tool" and ban it entirely. With nearly every student having at least one internet-connected device on a network not controlled by the school in their pocket, this "solution" makes no sense to me at all. In fact, the only thing we do when we ban tools like this is ban them for our students who are the most in need of educational resources; everyone else will still have access.

This kind of thinking widens our digital divide every time we act on it. Because, as long as I have a smartphone, I can turn off Wi-Fi and access ChatGPT to my heart's content anyway. I could easily share the text it generated in a hundred ways with myself and get it into the word processing software of my choice. And, shocking to many, the text generated by tools like this is *not plagiarized* in the strictest sense of the word. It is new text that has never been seen before; it just was not generated with a human brain, which to me is no different from the graph created by the latest TI calculator required for that upper-level math class. I still have to know what data to put in to get the desired results, and hopefully, have the knowledge, background, and skills to evaluate and refine those results. That last sentence took 45 seconds to write, but the skills I described are as complex as the ability to write the thing itself. One type of work impresses us: the ability to write the thing, and the other we automatically discount: the ability to evaluate and edit the thing, but the emergence of these technologies leaves us asking: why is one set of skills more valuable than the other? (And also, thanks to Allan Montford of Sarah Gould Consulting, and Tom Dinise of Wiley Publishing, and all of the other editors of this book, without whose skills it would not exist.)

It will take decades for our school's curriculum and our states' standards to catch up to a technology that was introduced in 2022, there is no doubt about that, but the wonderful thing about educators is that they have the intellectual ability to catch up much faster than state or even local entities can adapt. We can adapt today, right this second. Let's dive into how AI can and should change what we do in the classroom in a school where we, the educators, have the freedom to make adjustments to the world around us, which I hope, however unrealistic, is every classroom.

Pivoting into AI

An assignment my students and I loved when I was teaching was taking something complex and not meant for children and recreating it as a children's book. This was fun (and funny) for so many things we read and studied in class. It led to really interesting conversations about the writing and deep understanding of the literature we were addressing. For example, when I taught junior (11th grade) English, we read and rewrote for children the famous sermon "Sinners in the Hands of an Angry God" by Johnathan Edwards. The idea of rewriting a piece for a new audience is that you have to think about the piece of writing, what it means, who the audience is, and then you have to separate all of those elements and change just one thing, the audience. When the audience is a 3rd grader, what changes? The writer must decide, and that is a fun and often funny task, one ChatGPT could do in its spare time (it won't —I asked it to—because the themes of the sermon are considered "inappropriate for children," but you get the point). In the original sermon, Edwards begins, "The God that holds you over the pit of hell, much as one holds a spider or some loathsome insect over the fire, abhors you, and is dreadfully provoked." Now, if the 3rd graders are never actually going to read and be terrified by the book we're writing, we can really have a good time, and in this case, I would suggest they are imaginary instead of a real audience. In any case, it is abundantly clear that context matters when we're learning, and even if this one is imaginary, it helped us understand, discuss, and create in new ways with new enthusiasm which simply did not exist without it.

I recommended this strategy another time to a high school biology teacher who was working with her students on aquatic science. Here are some standards that could be addressed through an assignment like the one I'm remembering: "analyze interrelationships among producers, consumers, and decomposers in a local aquatic ecosystem; and identify the interdependence of organisms in an aquatic environment such as in a pond, river, lake, ocean, or aquifer and the biosphere."[4] In this case, high school students were learning these concepts, but lacked a context for making connections. Another way of saying this is that most of the students just didn't care; it's a common problem that I'm sure we are all too familiar with. Once the teacher introduced the idea that they would need to teach these concepts to other students, namely, a group of 2nd graders at a nearby elementary school, the important discussions around what the ideas really meant began to take shape. When she added in the information that many of the students they would be teaching came from homes where students did not own a single book, the high school students decided they would make books for their students and that every student would receive a book when they met up, which had already been planned. I spoke to a parent of a student in the class who completed this project and she told me that she normally struggled to get her son to even admit when he had homework, but during this project, he consistently worked from home and took supplies from home to complete different parts of the assignment. She was amazed and impressed that with the added context of the 2nd graders and the lack of home-based reading materials, her normally lackadaisical son could become excited about science again. Luckily, he wasn't alone; the teacher reported record engagement in all of her classes that worked on the project.

It was a fun day for me when I got to observe the high school students reading their books to the elementary students with whom they were paired. The little kids asked great questions, and I think most of the high school students had a lot of ah-ha moments as they tried to discuss the concepts they'd written about with the younger students. But mostly, I believe that every one of the high school students who participated in that project really learned the standards in a way that they never would have with a worksheet, which by its very definition, removes all context and relationships from learning.

Reflection Activity

Now that you (hopefully) have a little better understanding of how a tool like AI could be used in the classroom, I want you to imagine how you could start using tools like these. What project have you worked on with students in the past where there was little to no buy-in due to a lack of interest in the content? How could you leverage a tool like ChatGPT to get the students to engage with the material in a new way? How might this type of activity unlock a new level of learning for your students that might not have been possible previously? Think big!

Strategies and Tools for Improvement

Another consideration for how to implement tools like ChatGPT or other generative AI tools is by allowing them to do some of the grueling work you have to do as a teacher. Just to prove a point, I took a piece of writing I use as an example from my Google Drive (you can see it here https://fried.tech/bw-essay-example) and put it into ChatGPT with this prompt: "Grade this 11th-grade student essay on a 100-point scale. Mark mistakes and make suggestions for improving the essay. Compliment the writer on what he did well and inspire him to continue writing and working on the piece." I just used Ctrl/Cmd+A in the essay document to select all, Ctrl/Cmd+C to copy and Ctrl/Cmd+V to paste the essay right into the prompt space within the website http://chat.openai.com. Within seconds, I got this feedback for my fictional student "Manny." In the following text, the italic words are my "take" on what ChatGPT produced; the non-italicized text is pasted directly from the tool.

Essay Feedback

Overall, Manny's essay shows a heartfelt and engaging narrative about his experience with his first car. However, there are some areas for improvement to make the essay even stronger. *(I'm really impressed with the humanistic way this statement is made; it's something I would have said.)*

Punctuation and Grammar: There are some punctuation and grammar errors throughout the essay that need to be addressed. For example, there should be a comma before the dialogue tag in the first paragraph. Additionally, the second paragraph could benefit from proper punctuation to enhance readability. *(True and things I remarked on within this essay as well.)*

Sentence Structure: Manny's essay could benefit from varying sentence structures to create a more fluid and dynamic flow. Some sentences are short and choppy, while others are longer. Strive for a balanced mix of sentence lengths to maintain reader engagement. *(Good advice and also true.)*

Clarity and Transition: In some places, the essay lacks clarity and smooth transitions between ideas. For example, the shift from talking about the car to becoming an adult could be better connected to make the progression more evident. *(Wow, yes, great actionable feedback.)*

Paragraph Structure: The essay could be organized into distinct paragraphs to make it more visually appealing and to better group related ideas together. *(Once again, I can't argue with this advice, and if this essay were to be rewritten for improvement, this would be a crucial part of the rewrite.)*

Vocabulary: Although the essay has a personal tone, incorporating more descriptive language and specific details could enhance the reader's understanding and emotional connection to the story. *(Shockingly on point and... human-like advice.)*

Dialogue Formatting: Ensure that the dialogue is properly formatted with each new speaker's words starting on a new line. *(Yes, this addresses the biggest technical error I see in this writing.)*

Conclusion: The essay could benefit from a stronger conclusion that reflects on the significance of the experience and its impact on Manny's life. *(Also true and correct and a little scarily spot on.)*

Based on the rubric, here is the breakdown of the essay's strengths and areas for improvement: *(Note: I pasted in a rubric with the essay. I actually didn't realize it was in there because I didn't scroll to the second page when using Ctrl+A (select all), but I'm leaving this here because if you're really going to use ChatGPT, you should know about this capability to paste in a rubric with text.)*

- Ideas and Content: 22.5/25 (Strong)—The narrative effectively conveys Manny's excitement and experiences with his first car. *(Even taking the time to write this feedback showing an understanding of the topic takes so long for teachers to do. What if I could read the essay myself but use ChatGPT or another AI tool to write all of this? Pretty amazing thought.)*

- Voice: 25/25 (Strong)—Manny's personal voice shines through, adding authenticity to the essay.
- Organization: 13.5/15 (Effective)—The essay is organized well, but smoother transitions between ideas could be included.
- Sentence Fluency: 13.5/15 (Effective)—There is a good mix of sentence structures, but further improvement could be made to enhance flow.
- Word Choice: 9/10 (Developing)—The essay could benefit from more varied and descriptive vocabulary.
- Conventions: 9/10 (Developing)—Some punctuation and grammar errors need to be addressed, along with proper dialogue formatting.

Final Score: 93/100

Suggestions for Improving the Essay:

- Carefully proofread the essay to correct punctuation, grammar, and formatting errors.
- Consider breaking the essay into distinct paragraphs to enhance readability and organization.
- Add more descriptive language and sensory details to immerse the reader in the experience.
- Reflect on the significance of the car experience and its impact on Manny's growth as a person in a more developed conclusion.
- Reorganize the narrative to create smoother transitions between ideas and themes.
- Revise sentence structures to achieve a more balanced and engaging flow.

By addressing these suggestions, Manny's essay will become an even more compelling and well-crafted narrative.

(If I were really using AI to generate feedback for a student, I would now ask this of it: "Rewrite all of this exact same feedback to Manny himself as if you are the teacher." Then I would change my initial prompt to include the directive to the AI: "You are an 11th-grade English teacher" so that I wouldn't have to do this second step each time.)

If you are someone who tends to be afraid of change, I have likely just scared the bejesus out of you. The results it just took you several minutes to read were generated in mere seconds and sound remarkably human, the things I would write to a student if I had 30 minutes to grade an essay. Meanwhile, this entire process of getting the paper "graded" took less than 60 seconds. I can now, theoretically, copy and paste the entire response from ChatGPT back into Manny's paper and record that grade in the grade book; talk about "cheating," wow. Is it still cheating if you are the teacher? Asking for a friend (it's me, I'm the friend).

This example was provided not to suggest this is the best use of generative AI in your position as a teacher, but more to push the problem back the other direction. If you have a pain point, for example, excessive hours outside the classroom grading, and AI can solve that problem for you, is it "cheating" to change the way you address the issue or is it just working smarter? When you think of things this way, then apply the logic you'll use for your own position to students: is how they will use the tool then "cheating," or are we forced to look at the situation in new ways? It can get a little uncomfortable, can't it?

One thing I know for sure, the days of students working for weeks on end outside the classroom to turn in a long piece of writing should be over as of today. Even though you will know whether or not your student produced that work in front of you based on their previous work, you will not be able to prove an AI tool was used because the text you will be looking at will not be plagiarized, which by definition means that it is not original text. Text generated by AI tools IS original text. There are many tools that claim to be able to spot AI text with alarming accuracy, but they can't prove it, and their claims are in the company's interest and not the customer's. The only way to prove plagiarism is to find text from another source to match the text to; since text written by AI is generated from scratch, this cannot be done. I have read at least a dozen credible stories from students and even advanced academics who have been accused of using AI in their writing based on one plagiarism detection system or another who submit they did no such thing. The onus will be on schools to prove it, as it must be, and schools simply cannot. Can you use AI for this? I asked ChatGPT how to tell if it wrote work submitted by a student. After a few tries to get at exactly what I was asking, I learned that beyond using your human brain, at least as of the writing of this book, there is no way to tell. From this point forward, all writing assignments (or presentation creation, or many, many other tasks that generative AI tools can easily do in seconds) should be completed in class and version history or similar software tools must be used to determine whether the writing was done over time by a student or pasted in from AI. Even tools purchased to spot plagiarism cannot reliably tell which text was "written" by AI versus student-generated.

So, using version history in Google Docs, how can a teacher tell if text was pasted in from another source? Figure 11.3 shows what you will see in human-generated text. There are small changes over a long time, the color-coded pieces are connected to a minute-by-minute record of what was typed at that point in time.

With AI generated text (Figure 11.4), the color-coded text all appears at one moment in time, it's one block of

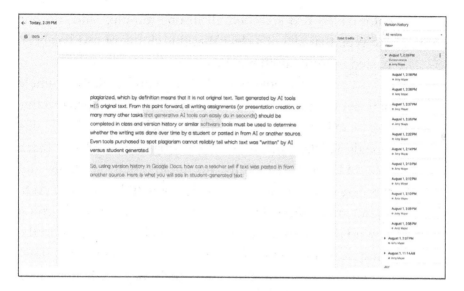

FIGURE 11.3 Identification of human-generated text.

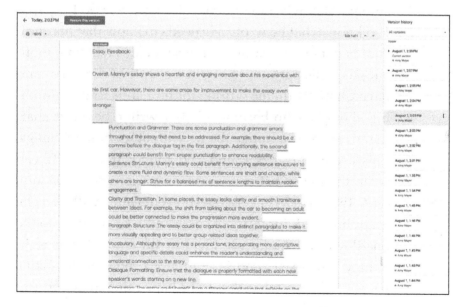

FIGURE 11.4 Identification of pasted text.

color-coded text stamped all in one minute. Since no one can type that fast, it's clear that this chunk of text has been pasted in from another source.

AI poses a whole new challenge and equally a whole new set of opportunities for educators who choose to live like it exists. I've seen T-shirts proclaiming, "Teach like Google Exists," and now a new slogan is needed: "Teach like AI Exists." Hopefully, eventually, both students and teachers can learn to leverage the incredible power of AI to spend more time doing the important work of learning how to do things computers will never be able to do in the extraordinary amount of time they can recoup from allowing computers to do things at which they are better—like, apparently, grading papers.

The other side of this coin, though, has to do with my student Manny's motivation. I still need to read his paper and know what he wrote. He needs to know that his audience is not just a computer or else there is really no motivation on his part not to key in a couple of sentences and have ChatGPT do the writing for him, thus learning nothing about how to become a better writer, better at sharing his story as a human being with other human beings. This argument goes round and round. If ChatGPT can write the paper better than Manny, why should Manny write the paper? That is a question educators will likely be grappling with for years to come and takes us back to the one day of calculator use I had in 4th grade. If this technology now exists and is ubiquitous, how do the skills we need change what should be happening in our education systems?

Takeaways

1. Massive world-changing technologies *should* change the way we educate students, but their impact is not always what we want to see or what would be most helpful for our students' futures. We have a unique opportunity to get it right this time by refusing to teach like AI doesn't exist.

2. The process of learning is recursive and messy. We have to have many opportunities to get things wrong, receive feedback, and try again before we can fully understand something to the degree we can do something important with what we learned.

3. Dealing with AI and the changes it will introduce into our worlds will take all our human capacities being engaged, far beyond worrying about plagiarism. We must determine what our humanity means when computers can now do things we thought were uniquely human.

Notes

1. Roose, K. (2023, January 12). Don't ban ChatGPT in schools. Teach with it. *New York Times*. https://www.nytimes.com/2023/01/12/technology/chatgpt-schools-teachers.html

2. Minitel. (2023, October 9). Wikipedia. https://en.wikipedia.org/wiki/Minitel#cite_note-mikrobitti-7

3. Center for Applied Research in Educational Technology. (2012).

4. Texas Education Code: Chapter 112. Texas Essential Knowledge and Skills for Science, U.S.C. § 112.32 (2023). https://tea.texas.gov/about-tea/laws-and-rules/sboe-rules-tac/sboe-tac-currently-in-effect/ch112c.pdf

Becoming a Worksheet Killer

One of my best friends in college, Barb, had a friend she always complained about; let's call her Ashley. I asked her one time to give me a better example of how this other woman was being a "bad" friend. Barb reported that after briefly giving Ashley a rundown of the major events that had recently occurred in her life, Ashley said, "Okay, but let's talk about ME some more!" In the case of this chapter, though, we're going to turn the tables and talk about YOU some more instead of me. YOU are actually my favorite topic of all. As a person who has nearly made it to the end of this book, my first book and perhaps my only one, though time will tell, you are the person I care about the most. Now that I've (hopefully) made you think in new ways and question how learning takes place, you might be asking, "So . . . now what? How do *I* become a Worksheet Killer?!"

About YOU

Before we jump into answering this question, I'm going to make some positive assumptions about you: you are a dedicated educator, though you could be in any number of roles in our field; you really care about learning and you want to make a positive difference in the lives of others. You also understand some things about human nature, no matter the age or experience of the human in question. Humans crave being known, with all our quirks and divots understood, and we hope, loved, not in spite of our weirdness, but because of it. Worksheets don't give us the chance to be seen in the ways we need as humans, which creates a fundamental disconnect between us. This is the same reason that even though ChatGPT or Gemini can make lesson plans, they will never be able to produce the unique creativity of a human teacher who knows her students. Worksheets and computer-generated lessons and writing are bones without marrow, the veins without the necessary lifeblood that humanizes the learning experience. On the surface, they may look basically the same but the amazing, unique, and magical properties of life are not within, and we feel that.

A few months ago, I was asked to try out an AI "Teacher Tool" for lesson planning and to offer a review to the creators. What follows is the review I offered:

> I tried your AI tool again a couple of times this morning. First I did an 11th-grade English lesson for "Ethan Brand," a short story by Nathaniel Hawthorne. This is sort of a "trick" topic because literature is no longer taught in school for its own sake; it's used to learn other skills. For example, one might read the short story in order to examine something about the writer's craft or theme. But, obviously, no tech tool can know this. The lesson plan it created wasn't the worst thing I've ever seen, but a teacher teaching a short story this way would have missed an

opportunity. Still, it's done every day all day though not "good" or particularly successful teaching.

Second, I used a common skill from the language arts standards that's hard to teach: inferencing. Inferencing is not something that should be taught one time but as a part of everything all year long, but let's think of the lesson created as an introduction to the skill. The content generated could be useful IF the teacher really understands what context clues are and how to make inferences themselves; however, this may or may not be the case. What's generated would likely create a circular problem of telling the teacher to find a piece of literature and use "context clues" while possibly (probably) not really understanding (without a good example) what that term means. If I knew how to do this, I wouldn't need the tool to help me. If I need the tool to help me, I probably don't understand the skill. *[I wonder, dear reader, if this sounds familiar to anyone?]*

Good teaching starts with a standard that is clear, measureable, yet doesn't exist in isolation. It creates experiences students participate in that shape their learning. It involves practice in multiple ways so that students can make the necessary connections. The tool telling me to "give students a worksheet" or a quiz on inferencing isn't helpful to this process and may be harmful.

Another characteristic of good teaching is differentiation. For example, in one class of 30 children, in an average school, I will have several students who have some sort of intellectual disability and several who are intellectually gifted. All students must learn how to infer/understand and draw inferences, but they don't all have to learn at the same pace, with the same material, and they may not need to perform with the same level of mastery. As a teacher, I would tailor the reading materials and the performance indicators for the intellectual abilities of my students. Nothing in what the AI generated gives me any information how to do this or that I should do it.

Let's look at this as a brand-new teacher who is untrained. Could this tool be helpful, that is, better than nothing? Possibly, but probably not. The classroom management skills necessary to get a room full of average high school students to slog through independent reading of a piece of literature and then do worksheets about it would far outstrip the skills of an untrained teacher. They could try to execute the "Ethan Brand" lesson plan, but it would abysmally fail unless there were some extraordinary circumstances. There is nothing to engage the students with the content. There is no life or connection in the materials that would draw in any student. Is a brand-new teacher going to understand this? Well, they will soon enough understand that something has to be there to spark interest.

I am not sure if this is the kind of information you're looking for, but I sincerely hope it's helpful.

To their credit, these creators agreed that the complexities of a good lesson plan were beyond the AI's capabilities at this time. Likely, they always will be, though AI can be a great starting place and timesaver to teachers, to be sure, especially if they have the critical skills to refine their questions to create something better than my clumsy initial attempt.

Becoming a Worksheet Killer

To truly become a *Worksheet Killer*, you must start with developing an understanding of people and their unquantifiable motivations to learn and grow. It is invaluable to me to know that Erica is mainly interested in makeup and boys, but lives for making her father proud, which good report cards and positive notes home do for her. I chat with her every day about whatever she's changed in her look and ask about her current love interest. I wait, watch, and I notice when she grasps something new and then give her a sticky note scrawled in haste, "Erica: awesome job on that 10-minute essay from last Thursday. I had honestly never thought about that topic from the point of view you gave it and you opened my eyes. Thank you! —Ms. Mayer." Of course, these notes end up making it home to Dad EVERY time.

What Cory needs even more than thinking about taking a break from the endless stream of (sometimes clever, often not) jokes and commentary is to know he's noticed, seen, and heard by me. I make sure to give him time in class each day to try to make me laugh. Once I genuinely laugh, a sense of calm comes over both of us and we have at least 30 minutes to do something academic. Because of his past, Tony needs to know that someone at school thinks of him as a good, smart kid and not a screw-up who is always one step away from disciplinary placement. I talk to him only about work from my class, but I ask him what he thinks and understands. He only sees himself as a "good student" for one short hour a day, in my room, but that's all it takes. Today he's a highly successful business leader who no one would know was thought of as a "bad" kid with no future when he was in high school.

Being a Worksheet Killer is not one thing; it's a million things that no one who hasn't taught, and deeply cared about students, will understand. It's everything and nothing at the same time. It's seeing the humanity in your students, your administration, your colleagues, and sometimes, even the parents who trust you with their students each day.

It takes integrity and it demands integrity of those to whom it's given. It's not easy, far from it! It's nearly impossible to do inside a system that lacks respect for the staff that interact with students, but you can do it anyway, if you're ready. If you want to start today, no matter what grade level or subject matter you teach, I promise that you *can* do it. If your students are old enough to write, this can begin with a writing assignment. If not, it can also be done with a video assignment through something like Screencastify or Flip. Send students away from class today with a little slip of paper with something like this on it:

> Tomorrow, I'm going to ask you to tell me what makes you unique and different from everyone else on the planet. What do you love? What gets you excited and motivated? What is something you could talk about endlessly? There might be only one thing or there might be five. Think about this before tomorrow, and be prepared to answer in class. Your answer will remain between you and me unless you choose to share with others.

Then it's time for you to do the same thing (we should always be ready to match what we ask our students to do). Be prepared to answer this question for yourself as you ask your students to answer it for you, and then share your answers with them. As much as you're asking your students to show you their humanity, you must be ready to reveal yours to them. I know there are those who will say things like, "It's unprofessional!" or similar, but the truth is, if you're expecting to work with humans successfully, you will have to become one of them and not just an entity they are surprised to see in the grocery store (how many times has one of your students, especially if you teach a younger grade, just assumed you LIVED at school?!). As an English teacher, I had the good fortune of getting to know the humanity in my students constantly through their writing. The first writing assignment I would assign to a new class would be something like "tell me about a turning point in your life." Most students knew immediately what that was for them, but for some, conversations were in order to figure it out; these too helped me see my students' humanity and understand how they saw themselves. Of course, we had the passing of beloved grandparents, houses that had burned down, moves to other countries, but we also had realizing my family were the "haves," the "rich people" that everyone was talking about, or that I saw myself as a person who "nothing has ever happened to" or as someone who thought of myself as a "good" person when others didn't see me that way at all.

After I've established relationships with my students so that they know I see them as the unique, incredible, singular humans they are, anything is possible for them in their learning because a relationship of trust has been created. Now, when I say, "Shawn, you can absolutely do this. I know you put an engine back into a car and made it run, and compared to that, this stuff is going to be a cake walk for you," he knows I mean it, and what's more, he believes it himself. I see him. I understand something about him, and the confidence I have in him that he can do it imbues him with the same belief.

Another equally important part of becoming the Worksheet Killer of your dreams is trusting your students and sometimes realizing that, no matter what you do, you cannot make another person learn if they don't want to. You can't blame yourself for that. I'm not suggesting that you stop trying and just give up when a student shows they don't want to learn. What I am saying is that you have my express permission to take yourself off the hook and trust that creating more engaging work will hook the maximum number of students possible into learning. Just know that this number will never be 100%. Now, 100% of your students WILL learn something, but 100% of your students will not learn 100% of what you want them to and what you attempt to teach them. That is impossible in a compulsory system because by our nature, many humans rebel against compulsory systems (in a way, I am asking you to do this yourself by becoming a Worksheet Killer). This is one reason why mentally removing yourself from total responsibility can actually "hook" more students. When I stopped trying to hound kids into turning in their worksheets, made them reliant on each other for their learning, and took my hands off the proverbial wheel, MORE students, not fewer, did their work. Meanwhile, I worked less and they learned more. While this sounds impossible, it's absolutely true. (And you know this because you read my stories.)

Unspoken Messages Are Often Louder than Spoken Ones

Think about human motivation in terms of that old software everyone once used that gave kids points for reading books. If you used it, whether as a teacher or as a student, you probably remember whether you got to host or go to the "pizza party" reward you could earn by reading books of a certain point value, then taking short, plot-based quizzes on them through a rudimentary computer program. The result of that software was that thousands (millions?) of students got this message:

- Rewards are only given for things that other people want me to do that I do not want to do, for example, eating vegetables that I don't like or want to eat gets me cake, and reading books is so horrible, they have to give me pizza afterward to get me to do it.

- Things that are actually fun, like going to the swimming pool in the summer, are their own reward and no prizes, games, or tracking are necessary; no prizes for going swimming, prizes for reading books and eating vegetables. Got it! Reading books and eating vegetables are bad; pizza, cake, and prizes are good, and thus, are classified as rewards.

- Therefore, if a reward is offered, it's because the activity itself isn't intrinsically rewarding.

- Finally, reading is a task or chore that no one wants to do; therefore, in order to get people to do it, an extrinsic reward must be offered.

Millions of people were inadvertently taught that reading is dull, arduous, difficult, or otherwise to be avoided because prizes were offered for doing it. Meanwhile, school officials were talked into believing that reading scores would go up because of all of the extra reading that would be going on because of the gamified system. If anything of the sort had proved true, there would have been thousands of these programs and they would still be in ubiquitous use today. Alas, like so many strategies tried in educational settings, the message came through to the humans involved, intentionally shared or not.

My message that I do my best to make sure I relay clearly and consistently to my students is this: I care about you very much and I'm giving you learning experiences that I believe will make you a stronger and better reader, writer, thinker, and community member. I deeply believe the skills I want you to learn will matter for the rest of your life. I have done my part to consider how to create a system in my classroom that will motivate and inspire you, where you can work with others and learn to depend on teammates as they will learn to depend on you. But, I cannot care overly much about whether you take me up on the opportunity. As I let go of the idea that it was up to me whether people learned or not, they took over the desire at the same rate I was able to let it go. It was almost as if as I continued carrying the weight of it, they felt they didn't have to, but the truth is, as long as I carried it for them, they were never going to be able to carry it themselves. (Hashtag irony.)

With these skills, decisions, and qualities I'm suggesting to you, authenticity is *incredibly* important. One thing I love about students is that they almost always know when educators are "faking it." Now, I told you when I began the Panthera Project, I did pretend *not* to care. That turned out to be effective, but the emotions I had about caring about and believing in the work I was asking students to do were completely genuine, and that matters. It actually doesn't matter that much whether I'm the world's best lesson designer or curriculum disaggregator, but more whether the skills students are practicing are skills they need to have to be successful in their lives as students or just as citizens of the world. For example, I feel so good about knowing that I gave students the opportunity to learn to work interdependently in my classroom because I am certain that skill is valuable to them to this day. This is the real way we Kill the Worksheet.

Begin at the Beginning

So how do you begin? I hate to say it, but there isn't a universal answer here, no "trick" that will magically make this work. You will begin by finding out what makes your students uniquely human, which will change from class to class and year to year. Study these unique traits and experiences, remember them, and then show your students that you not only know this information, but that it is deeply important to you. Figure out the same for yourself and make all the connections you can. Ask your students about how they learn and what they think, and really listen to what they say. Show them and tell them how you are adjusting instruction to connect with them on a daily basis.

Then what? Well, again, unfortunately there is no "one-size-fits-all" cut-and-dried answer, but if you cared enough to get to the end of this book, I think the answer is closer than you may think. Try something out, steal my ideas and make them your own, find new crazier ideas that work better than I could have ever hoped, and beyond everything else, never stop trying. Your students will know if you've given up on them, so don't. Give yourself the same freedom I've asked you to give your students to fail and try again. I believe in you, your students believe in you, so take the leap and believe in yourself. This is how you kill the worksheet.

Final Takeaways

1. Only teachers who care can kill worksheets; the change starts with you.

2. Thinking through unspoken messages is a powerful practice. Students, especially teenagers, are experts at recognizing and rebelling against hypocrisy, so examine systems of reward and punishment carefully for unintended messages.

3. Recognizing the humanity in your students and allowing them to recognize the humanity in you is essential to making the human connections necessary to finally, actually Kill the Worksheet.

A Word to the Readers from Amy

I am so grateful to you for reading this book. I sincerely hope that it comes through to you as a work of heart, because that's what it has been for me. When I was a few chapters from finishing the first draft, I picked up another education-focused book that was about AI. After I read two chapters of it, I decided the entire thing must have been written by AI. It lacked any personality or punch. I decided then and there, even before I heard back from my awesome editor, that I would not be persuaded to "calm it down" or be more serious in this book. Whether you loved it or hated it, at least it would be authentic.

As I wrote, I got teary-eyed remembering many of the students and stories in this book, and the lessons those students taught me that were undoubtedly so much more poignant and powerful than anything I likely taught them. If what's between the covers here connected with you, I hope you will encourage other educators to read it too. The very best recommendation that could be given to this book is from one teacher to another. I also want to encourage you to learn with friEdTech, my company that is filled with former public school educators who now work to create engaging learning experiences for educators. Much of our work is produced for companies like Google, Adobe, Figma, Newsela, Intuit, and so many more. We make sure that when you are learning how to use these products in a classroom setting, your own learning is as engaging, meaningful, and well-designed as it can be. We also work directly with schools to help them organize and implement their goals for improving or even transforming the culture of learning. You can find out more about friEdTech on our website, http://fried.tech, and you can subscribe to our newsletters here: http://fried.tech/subscribe. Another interesting place to read more is our blog found here: http://fried.tech/blog or our social media, just search for friEdTech on any platform you use. We get the most traction on Facebook at http://fried.tech/ft-fb.

Another thing I'd love you to remember is that there are a ton of resources in this book for you to use; look for the short URLs like those just listed, but even more importantly, we have an entire online school you can become a member of so that you can continue your learning at your own pace. Through a friEdOnline membership, learn more at http://friEdOnline.com, you will get ready-made templates you can use immediately and carefully designed experiences that will help you manage your workload, classroom, and generally improve your practice all around. Hopefully, you trust me by now, so that when I tell you it's like no other online learning you've done before, you are encouraged to check it out for yourself. Our end user ratings are around 4.5 out of 5, which is totally unheard of for online learning.

If you prefer in-person learning or would like to have me present at your school in a keynote session, please fill out the contact form found here: http://fried.tech/contact. I would love to meet you and your educational community in person wherever you are in the world!

Sincerely,

Amy

Acknowledgments

First, I am grateful to Allin Montford, whose dedication and meticulous revising and editing were instrumental in bringing this book to fruition. His support and enthusiasm not only kept me on track, but also nurtured a friendship. (Allin, remember when you had to read what I had written so far because you didn't know if you wanted to help me!?! Thanks for saying, "Yes.")

I also extend my heartfelt thanks to my colleagues at friEdTech, especially Jessica Powell-Allbright. Her enthusiasm and encouragement after reading the initial chapter was pivotal in motivating me to continue this writing journey. (Will she read the rest of it? Only time will tell!—there will be an assessment later. Just kidding. Sort of.)

Special thanks to Alicia Swedberg and Brooke Lowery, whose exceptional talent in graphics and design significantly enhanced the visual appeal and functionality of this book. Their contribution has made the templates and graphics both user-friendly and aesthetically pleasing. (Brooke, the TTWWADI Monster is even better than the original!)

Finally, my profound gratitude to my husband, Rich. While the method behind my madness might sometimes elude him, his unwavering support and belief in me have been my constant source of strength and encouragement. His presence has been a cornerstone in this endeavor and every other one in my adult life. Rich, thank you for always being there supporting me and for helping me shape ideas found in this book.

To each of you acknowledged, I offer my sincere thanks. Your support and belief in me and this project have been invaluable to me as a writer and teacher.

About the Author

Amy Mayer, the visionary behind friEdTech, is a celebrated figure in the educational technology landscape. Beginning her career in classrooms near Houston, Texas, Amy has evolved into a national authority in education and technology. Her dual expertise in English and foreign language education, coupled with her innovative approach as a campus and district leader in instructional technology and staff development, has profoundly shaped her professional trajectory.

Amy's academic path at Sam Houston State University, culminating in a Master of Arts in English with a focus on Technical Writing and Bachelor of Arts degrees in both English and French, started her journey to becoming an entrepreneur and leader in edtech.

Amy's tenure at Conroe ISD was marked by her innovative leadership, particularly through the WOW! Academy, a program created to help teachers effectively and meaningfully integrate online tools while promoting student-centered learning. It was through the success of WOW! Academy that Amy began to understand the profound impact of challenge-based and project-based learning on student outcomes and witnessed the transformations in classrooms as teachers left behind worksheets in favor of experiential learning. She also served for two Texas state agencies as a language arts and a curriculum and instruction consultant, then, as a Director for Staff Development and District Initiatives, and later, returned to her first love, instructional technology, as a director for the largest private school in Houston.

As an adjunct professor, Amy extended her influence to higher education, teaching at both Lone Star College and Sam Houston State University. Her educational initiatives were not confined to her own classrooms; she has organized and presented countless hours of educator professional development, and now owns and runs a company that has exponentially amplified this work serving teachers through partnerships with state departments of education, specifically in the entire state of Mississippi, for a multiyear contract to provide professional development, and with companies like Google, Adobe, Newsela, Figma, Intuit, and many others for synchronous and asynchronous learning that teachers enjoy nationwide.

Amy founded her company, friEdTech, an education technology professional development organization, which employs two dozen former teachers, campus and district coordinators, and administrators. Her company's learning experiences are known for their engagement, practicality, and relevancy for immediate and lasting impact to the classroom. friEdTech strives to provide educators with strategies for teaching that avoid lower-order thinking activities (such as worksheets) in favor of interactive and collaborative learning options that facilitate stronger critical thinking. Amy is well-known for her philosophy that effective learning should be as enjoyable and memorable as it is educational.

Amy's journey from a classroom teacher to a national speaker and professional development (PD) provider in educational technology is a testament to her passion for transforming education. She continues to inspire educators across the country with her dynamic approach to professional learning, proving that with the right blend of technology and creativity, the possibilities in education are limitless.

Explore More with Amy at: http://fried.tech | Facebook: friEdTechnology Instagram: friEdTech

About the Author

Index

Page numbers followed by *f* refer to figures.

A

Active slides, 38–41, 98

Actual model of learning, 228*f*

Admission, review, and dismissal (ARD), 69, 71

Adobe, 259

Adobe Express, 22

Adult-centered environments, 9*f*, 10–11

Adult-centered learning environments, 91

Allen, Kelly-Ann, 147

Animoto, 78

Artificial intelligence (AI):
  challenges of, 244
  in essay writing, 239
  generating feedback with, 240
  identifying, 241–242, 243*f*
  implementing, 238
  as learning tool, 38
  pivoting into, 235–237
  and prompt engineering, 230
  review of, 248, 250
  as rubric, 111
  ubiquity of, 231
  as worksheet killer, 217–237

Ashe, Arthur, xi

Assessment:
  of at-home work, 29
  in centered classrooms, 108, 110
  in collaborative learning, 84
  formative, 139
  grading as, 111
  as part of teaching cycle, 51
  standardized, 9, 28
  in teacher-focused classrooms, 95
  testing as, 49
  worksheets as, 30–31

Assignment building, 107

Asynchronous learning, 16

At-risk students, 9, 11, 13, 92

Atwood, Margaret, 6

B

Bard, 111, 231, 248

Behavior, 133–147
  and belief, 74
  -challenged students, 54
  change in teacher, 71–72
  discussing, 192
  and engagement, 138–139

267